Good Morning Mr. Lion

65 Orff-based
Music and Movement Activities
YOU can do TODAY!
Ages 3-6 years

Nicole Hammer

Illustrated by Sandy Reid

DEDICATION

This book is an ode to the diverse talents of children and their power to grow creatively. And to the teachers who help them find what they love to do and let them do it in their own way.

I also dedicate this book to my husband Richard who so many years ago had the generosity, and foresight to order a complete set of Orff instruments, even though he knew very little of Orff Schulwerk. This set the course for my career in which he has always acted as my staunchest supporter, believing in me more than I did myself at times. Thank you, Richard, for always being there.

Noor, 8 years old (home-schooled bilingual French-English)

Copyright © 2014 Nicole Hammer, California. All Rights Reserved.

Printed in the U.S.A. No part of this publication may be reproduced, stored in a retrieval system or transmitted, in any form, electronic, mechanical, photocopying, recording, or otherwise, without the prior written permission of the publisher: 2415 San Ramon Valley Blvd, Suite 4308, San Ramon Ca, 94583

For further information, go to: www.NicolesMusicClass.com
Cover Design: Richard Hammer
Cover Artwork: Sandy Reid
Photographs: Dominique Zenner, Ine Wallaert, Family Archives, Richard Hammer, Louise Buitenhuis
Editor: Peter Greenwood
Book design and Typesetting: Bill Holab Music
ISBN: 978-0-9863800-1-3

TABLE OF CONTENTS

Foreword	2
Introduction	4
The Basic Tenets of Orff Schulwerk	6
I. RHYMES	8
I.1 COUNTING RHYMES	8
One, Two, Tie My Shoe	8
I.2 COUNTING-OUT RHYMES	11
Skinty Tinty	11
Eeny Meeny Miney Mo	14
I.3 RHYMES ABOUT BIRDS	16
One Day a Turkey Came Out for a Walk	16
Once I Saw a Little Bird Go Hop, Hop, Hop	20
I.4 HALLOWEEN RHYMES	25
Five Little Witches	25
I.5 TRAIN RHYMES	28
Engine, Engine, Number Nine	28
I.6 FOOD RHYMES	31
Pat-a-Cake	31
Mix a Pancake	34
What's Your Favorite Food?	37
I Like Choc'late sauce	38
Guess the Food Word Played on the Drum	39
I.7 A COMPLETE MUSIC AND MOVEMENT PROJECT BASED ON CATS AND MICE	41
Five Little Mice	41
Pussycat, Pussycat, What do you Want?	43
His Majesty's Cat	44
The Mouse's Husband	45
Pussy Came Parading	48
Listening to "Cat Music"	50
Art Project	50
II. MOVEMENT AND LISTENING GAMES	52
Red Rover	53
Walk to the Drum	56
Move to the Sound of the Instruments	56
Moving with Objects	57
III. SONGS	60
Up and Down, Up and Down	61
Pop Up Game	62
Who Has the Walnut?	63
Out in My Garden	65
Rain, Rain, Go Away	66

    Postman 68

    Jason Wears a Red Shirt 71

    On My Head is a Little Bonnet 72

    To Stop the Train 75

    Suggested Songs for Pre-School, Kindergarten and First Grade 76

IV. DANCING 79

  IV.1. DANCING TO A SONG 79

    TRADITIONAL AMERICAN SONGS 79

      Shoo Fly 80

      Jump Jim Joe 81

    SONGS FROM OTHER COUNTRIES 82

      L'inverno l'è Passato 82

      Frère Jacques 84

      San Isidro Labrador 85

      Sharpen Your Knives and Scissors 90

    SONGS BASED ON STORIES 92

      Thorn Rosa 93

      Making Capes for Thorn Rosa, the Prince and the Wicked Witch or Wizard . . . 95

    SONGS FROM THE AFRO-AMERICAN HERITAGE 98

      Little Johnny Brown 98

  IV.2. DANCING TO RECORDED MUSIC 100

    CLASSICAL MUSIC 100

      The Princess and the Goblin 100

      Papillons (Butterflies) 102

    DANCE MUSIC COMPOSED FOR CHILDREN 104

      Highway no. 1 104

      Les Saluts 104

    MUSIC FROM AROUND THE WORLD 105

      Kukuvicka 105

      La Torototelle 106

      Carnavalito 107

    ACTIVITIES BASED ON A STORY 108

      The Lion Who Saw Himself in the Water 108

      Good Morning Mister Lion 109

      Introduction and Royal March of the Lions 111

EPILOGUE 113

BIBLIOGRAPHY AND DISCOGRAPHY 115

ABOUT THE AUTHOR 117

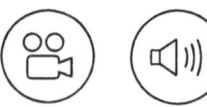

These symbols indicate there are Audio or Video versions of the activities at our website: http://membersite.NicolesMusicClass.com

ACKNOWLEDGEMENTS

Man cannot invent. He can only observe and discover, analyze, repeat and rearrange. We fit together the signs and clues from the world around us and from these we make something new.

—Jehudi Menuhin

My gratitude to all the wonderful, dedicated teachers who have made it possible for me to learn my craft and build a curriculum by going to their workshops, reading their books, watching their videos and following their training courses.

I thank my husband, Richard, for the video and audio recordings and help with all things electronic. Thanks also to my daughter, Ine, for the first round of editing and to Peter Greenwood, my editor, for his critical (and musical) eye, and for his skill at transforming my "Fleminglish" into a more readable text.

Thanks to Dominique Zenner for her beautiful pictures of Ghent, to Dilek Seren for her collaboration on videos and suggestions for children's books, to Louise, Noor and Artus for their beautiful art work and Sandy Reid for her wonderful book cover and illustrations.

A heartfelt thanks to Hans for having given me love and shelter when I needed it most, to my friend Bruce Reid who made sure I kept my feet on the ground and my head pointed in the right direction and to my daughters Annik and Ine who helped me grow up.

FOREWORD

This testimonial, which I think makes a fine foreword, was written in 1988 by Alyson Wade, who was 7 at the time. She came to my house on Friday afternoon with her friend Kelly for a weekly music class which quickly turned into a cozy afternoon enjoyed by all three of us. One day she gave me a booklet of type written text she had dictated to her Mom and a drawing of her hand on each page. It's one of the nicest testimonials I have and I am very happy to share it.

Nicole's by Alyson Wade
This book is dedicated to my favorite music teacher, Nicole

Every Friday I do something I really like. I go to my music lesson at Nicole's. Sounds boring, right? But it's not just a music lesson; it's much, much more.

Kelly, my music partner and I get to Nicole by bus #4. It's fun going on bus #4 because we like to talk and play with our friends. Kelly and I like to tease some boys on the bus.

After Kelly and I get there, Kelly, Nicole and I go to the store two blocks away. We can get candy, bubble gum, coke, and more good things to eat. We walk back to Nicole's and Kelly and I watch T.V. while Nicole makes some of her yummy and delicious muffins and French fries. Nicole calls us "the French fry monsters."

After we eat, we play our recorders. We play all kinds of songs. Nicole plays one thing, and then, Kelly and I repeat after her. We learn lots of notes. Sometimes we all play different parts at the same time.

Kelly and I learn dances from different countries. We do square dancing. All of us love to dance!

Nicole has tons of Orff instruments like: xylophones, wooden sticks that make soft sounds, drums, and tambourines. Kelly loves to play the drums. I love to play the xylophone.

All of us dress-up and dance to different pieces. We usually dress-up in long skirts and short tops. Kelly loves dressing-up in a top with pink bows on it and a skirt with two cherries on it.

We write puppet shows and act them out. We have music at our puppet show. Puppet shows are fun because puppets are fun.

I love to go to Nicole's because I love music, puppets, dress-up, dance, recorder, modeling, the bus ride, going to the store, Nicole and Kelly. I really like Nicole's yummy muffins and French fries. Nicole is very good teacher. If I had to vote for her on a scale of 1 to 100,000,000,000, she would break the scale by infinity.

INTRODUCTION

Good Morning, Mister Lion is the result of 45 years of teaching and creating musical activities for children. As I began to write down those activities I saw that my own evolution as a teacher and my enthusiasm for the spirit of Orff Schulwerk has roots in my childhood experiences growing up in Ghent, a jewel of a city in Belgium. So it felt quite natural to weave some of those memories into this tapestry of musical mice and lions, kings and queens.

I moved to California and began teaching music at the Laguna Beach Montessori School. Soon after, I attended a workshop given by Doug Goodkin, a renowned Orff Schulwerk teacher. Ten minutes into the class I knew this was my real home! Here was an enthusiastic and passionate person showing me an approach to teaching that made sense and was, at the same time, completely unfettered by academic notions of how children should learn.

The group activities Doug presented in that class covered movement, speech, body percussion, instruments, and singing and performing with props and costumes. At the end of it all, each group showed very different and even spectacular results. Soon after that I took the Orff Schulwerk training and understood that what had moved me so deeply was the joy that comes from putting together music, drama and dance pieces, from hearing and telling stories about the world and oneself, and how all this, when you shape it so that children can understand it and do it themselves, gives rise to the most wonderfully imaginative and creative moments.

I'll be telling you more about those days in Ghent as we work our way through this book but let me set the scene by describing the living room of our big house where many pictures hung on the walls and there was always music playing because my father was a great music lover, one of the first in town to own a gramophone player! In that room was a big, long table covered with projects of my dad's and my grandmother's. She had a knitting and corsetry store and used the table to draw her patterns, while Dad drew and painted, welded candelabras and lanterns, copied paintings of Bruegel with pieces of colored wood, manufactured his own Hawaiian guitar, and made us a puppet theatre.

On Friday nights, when Dad's musician friends came over to jam in our big living room, my sister and I would dress up and go all out with our choreography, hopping around the room with Mom, Dad playing his drum set as my sister and I sang "Pardon me boy, is that the Chattanooga choo choo?" long before we understood a word of English.

The basis of my work is the wonderful approach to teaching music called Orff Schulwerk. If this is your first encounter with Orff, here are some important points that will help you enter this world in the proper spirit.

THE BASIC TENETS OF ORFF SCHULWERK

Orff Schulwerk is an educational approach to music developed in Germany in the 1920s and 30s by composer Carl Orff and his colleague Gunild Keetman. The literal translation of schulwerk—school work—doesn't properly convey the open, creative spirit of this approach. Here are some of the most important principles, all of which you will find employed in this book.

- Children are naturally inclined to sing, dance, chant rhymes, clap and play a beat on anything they can find. As teachers we must use these natural impulses to learn music by first making it, then later learning how to read it.
- To link the music class to the natural tendencies of young students, the Orff teacher uses speech, movement, dance, singing, stories, drama, improvisation and instrumental playing as the framework of the program.
- Simple echo games and the use of short rhythmic patterns are basic techniques used to create a step by step approach to the development of musical skills. A key factor in this endeavor is improvisation. The choice of material must always be easy to understand but challenging enough to make the activity interesting.
- Music is a communal effort where children discover the joy of music-making with others. It is important for a child to know that working with other children who have different strengths results in creations that no individual could have imagined.
- The process is more important than the end result. A finished product need not be the goal because there are always endless possibilities.
- Stories and drama are key elements in the Orff music class. The power of drama invigorates the imagination of children, teaches them how to collaborate and strengthens their self-esteem.
- Orff Schulwerk also attaches much importance to music and dance from cultures around the world and these traditions are used as a means of bringing the children's attention to the importance of individual expression and creativity.

Finally, what distinguishes the Orff approach from traditional pedagogy is its emphasis on creativity. Creativity is about forming ideas, considering them and then refining them. This is what children do when they are asked to change the words of a rhyme or a song, change a story or look for different dance moves, postures or body percussion sounds. Singing, dancing, movement games, body percussion and instrumental playing involve physical processes that demand coordination of body and mind, feeling and intuition as nothing else can. Those activities stimulate the creative process. And, as everyone knows, children are happiest when they're singing and dancing, that is, creating, with each other.

I. RHYMES

I. 1. COUNTING RHYMES

One, Two, Tie My Shoe

One, two, tie my shoe
Three, four, shut the door
Five, six, pick up sticks
Seven, eight, lay them straight
Nine, ten, a big fat hen.

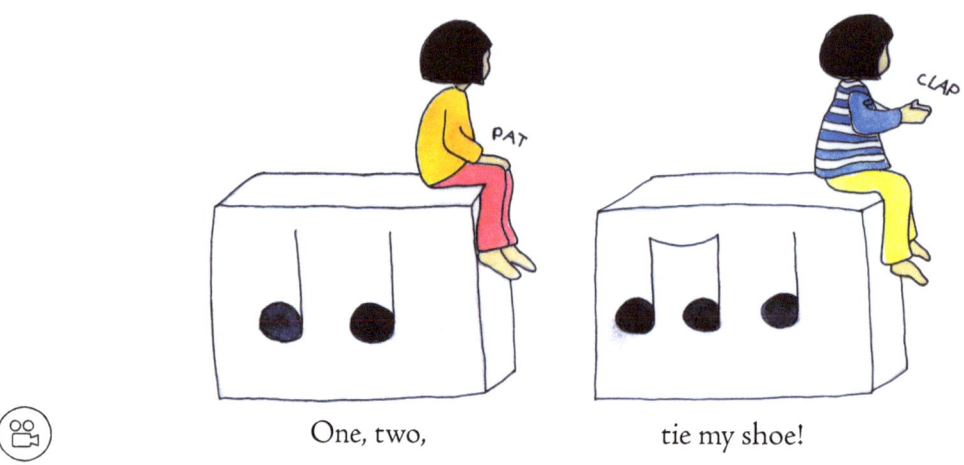

One, two,   tie my shoe!

This activity, based on a nursery rhyme, involves speech, movement, body percussion and instruments. It allows children to practice the concept of contrast and also expands their vocabulary.

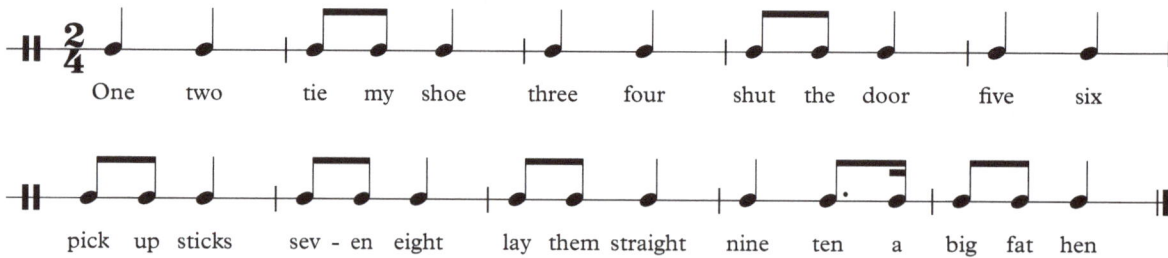

ACTIVITY (Preschool, Kindergarten and First Grade)

Children and teacher sit in a circle. Use the contrast between numbers and words to play the following activities:

SPEECH

- Say the numbers quietly and the words loud
- Say the numbers in a high voice, like a mouse, and the words in a low voice, like a giant
- Say the numbers in a happy (scared, pleading…) voice and the words in a sad (brave, commanding…) voice.

MOVEMENT
Find two different movements: one for the numbers and one for the words.
- Ex: *Hop* and *stamp*

BODY PERCUSSION
Find two contrasting sounds.
- By yourself: ex., *pat* and *clap*
- With a partner: ex., *clap your hands* and *clap your partner's hands*

INSTRUMENTS
Choose one instrument to play two different sounds.
- Ex: rhythm sticks tapped together and separately on the floor

Choose two different instruments.
- Ex: drum and wood block

Playing wood block and drum

Suggested Children's Book
Wood Audrey, Wood Dan. *Quick as a Cricket*. England. Child's Play International Ltd. 1982

A note about body percussion in Orff-Schulwerk
In Orff-Schulwerk an important tool for the exploration of musical structures is the one closest to us: our own body. Body percussion allows us to tap into our innate feeling for rhythm and prepares us for reading rhythmic notation. Once learned, it's fairly easy to transfer these gestures to un-pitched instruments.

Body percussion in Preschool, Kindergarten and First Grade is a combination of hand clapping, chest tapping, thigh patting and foot stamping. (Finger snapping is still a challenge.)
In this book:

- CLAP indicates clap hands
- CHEST indicates tap chest
- PAT indicates pat thigh
- STAMP indicates stamp foot

1.2. COUNTING-OUT RHYMES

Skinty Tinty

Skinty Tinty my black hen
Lays her eggs for gentlemen
Sometimes nine and sometimes ten
Skinty Tinty my black hen

🔊

Using a counting-out rhyme to determine who will start an activity is a very old custom. It is a much better solution than a random choice—the teacher is saved from having to single someone out. The children love it and consider it a game in itself.

In the traditional play form, one child counts the others out until only one remains. With very young children in a large group, it is usually the teacher who goes around once and points to each child in turn to the rhythm of the rhyme. The last person to be pointed at is IT.

A counting-out rhyme can also become an activity in itself as you will find out from the following games. There is a wealth of English counting-out rhymes in the wonderful books of Iona and Peter Opie.

This easy rhyme is one of the children's favorites. Use it with movement or body percussion and it becomes a great exercise for internalizing the feeling of meter and form in the whole body. This rhyme can be played in 6/8 or 4/4 meter. Most movements fit both meters except for skipping and galloping for which the natural choice would be 6/8. To make the activities accessible for all teachers, I have used both meters and added appropriate activities.

We start in 6/8, which gives me an excuse to introduce my old hobby horse who has been with me for as long as I've been working. He's retired now and rather happy about it because over the years he lost most of the mane he was so proud of. When the children were riding him it would float up and down with their movements and they loved that so much that they made a special effort to bounce as high as they could.

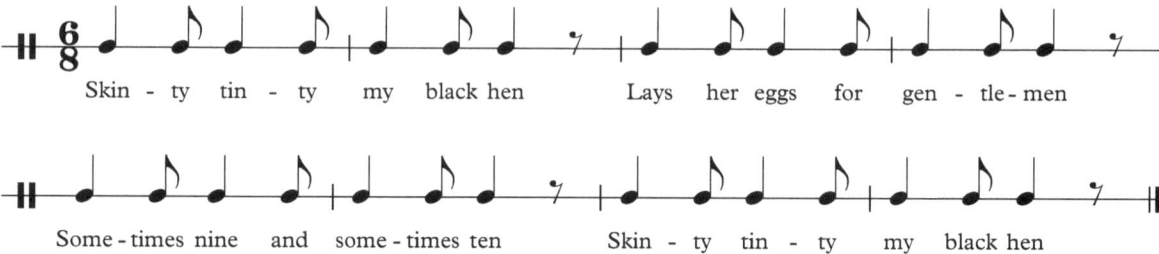

Activity in 6/8 (Preschool, Kindergarten and First Grade)

We use a hobby horse and a galloping rhythm played on a drum by the teacher to help internalize the rhythm of the rhyme.

The children and the teacher sit in a circle and learn the rhyme while they pat or clap to the beat.

Ask which characters appear in the rhyme (hen and the gentlemen).

Talk about the means of transportation in the days of this rhyme when there were no cars: how would a gentleman go to the farm to pick up his eggs? (On foot, by carriage or riding a horse.)

Even though carrying eggs while riding is not the safest way, it gives you an opportunity to introduce the hobby horse.

What are the different movements of a horse? (Walking, trotting, galloping and jumping.)

Show the children how to mount the hobby horse and ask them to ride around the circle while the other children guess the movement. (This way saves a child who doesn't know how to gallop from embarrassment.)

Teacher plays a galloping rhythm on the drum:

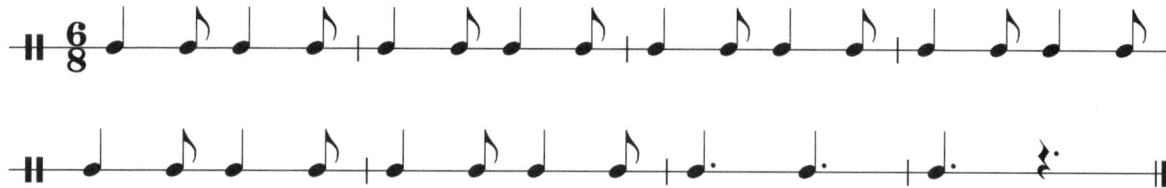

Recite the rhyme using the same movements and drum accompaniment in the following way:

Children and teacher sit in a circle with one child outside the circle on the hobby horse. Everyone speaks the rhyme while the child on the hobby horse waits. When the rhyme is finished, the teacher plays the galloping rhythm in 6/8 on the drum and the child chooses to gallop, walk, trot or jump around the circle. When finished the child passes the horse to another child and the game starts all over until everyone has had a turn.

Activity 1 in 4/4 (Preschool and Kindergarten)

In this activity we use body percussion and instruments to highlight the form of the rhyme: four identical phrases each ending with a rest. Clapping at the rest helps young children to hear it when it is placed at the end of a musical phrase.

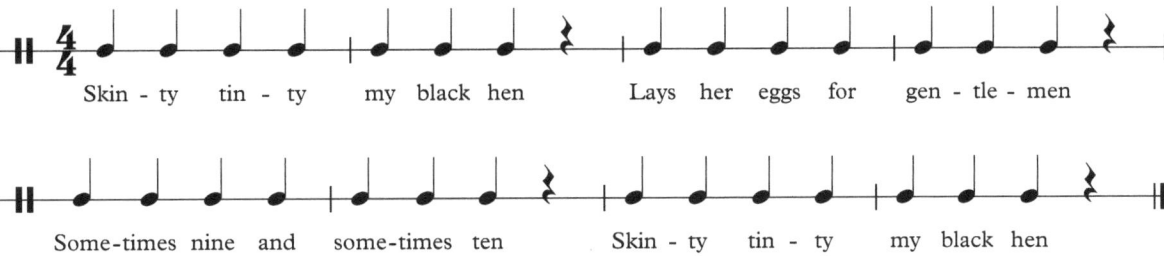

Teacher and children sit in a circle and accompany the rhyme with the following body percussion pattern: **Pat** on the words and **Clap** on the rests.

- Substitute body percussion with percussion instruments
- Rhythm sticks: Tap floor on the words and tap together on the rests.
- Other instruments: Invite the children to find two instruments with a contrasting sound, one for the words and the other for the rests.

Activity 2 in 4/4 (Preschool, Kindergarten)

The following activities use movement as the means to reinforce the feeling of form.

Ask the children to stand up and walk around the room while they are reciting the rhyme and clapping the rests. They have to be back in their spot at the end of the rhyme.

Change the walking into other movements, e.g:
- Hop on one leg and change to the other leg after each clap,
- Walk sideways and change direction after each clap.

They choose other movements.

Eeny Meeny Miney Mo

Eeny meeny miney mo,
Where did all the children go?
To the East, to the West,
To the one they love the best

This well known counting-out rhyme is an excellent opportunity for more body percussion work. We perform it together with movement and a special clapping activity which is particularly interesting because we cross our hands (crossing the midline). This type of movement is very useful for young children; among other advantages, it helps them with reading and writing. If this is too challenging, try alternating clapping your own hands with clapping your partner's hands.

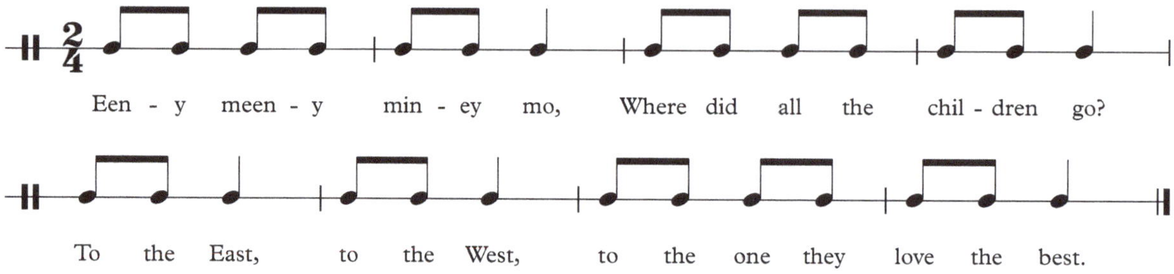

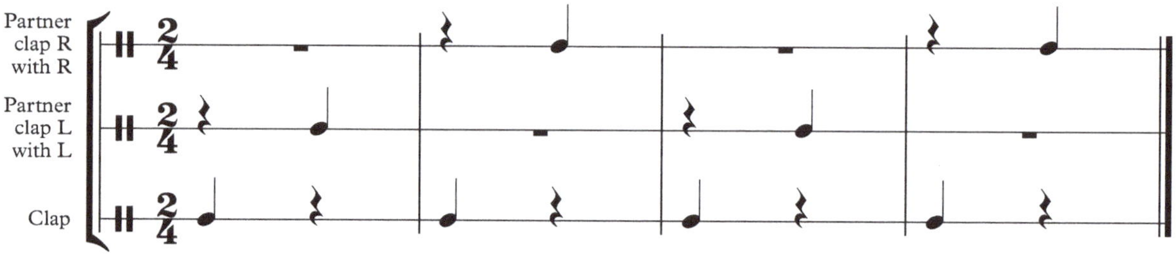

Een - y meen - y min - ey mo, Where did all the chil - dren go?
To the East, to the West, to the one they love the best.

Crossing the midline

Before you begin
Practice the clapping pattern before the game starts.

Let the children perform it by themselves, with an invisible partner in front of them. Emphasize that on the first "To" they have to clap their own hands. Once they get that they seem to have a much easier time with it.

When they are comfortable with the pattern, ask them to pair up with a friend and practice.

Activity (Kindergarten and First Grade)
- Standing in a circle, one child inside the circle. This child walks around when the rhyme starts and stops in front of another child on "go"
- Both perform the clapping pattern and at the end of the rhyme the new child steps inside the circle
- Both children now walk around by themselves when the rhyme starts again and at the next "go" they each find a new partner

The game continues, each time doubling the amount of children until all are playing

Eeny, meeny, miney, mo, where did all the children go?
(walk to the beat and stop in front of a child on "go")

To the (clap own hands)
East (clap partner's left hand with your left hand)
To the (clap own hands)
West (clap your partner's right hand with your right hand)

To the (clap own hands)
one they (clap partner's left hand with your left hand)
love the (clap your own hands)
best (clap your partner's right hand with your right hand)

Extension
Use this activity to change partners in any dance or game.

Partners separate at the end of the dance (or game) and walk around freely while saying the rhyme. Stop on "go" to do the clapping pattern with the one who is closest and becomes your new partner.

1.3. RHYMES ABOUT BIRDS

One day my daughter found a wounded pigeon and brought it to her grandparents. They nursed it back to health and carried it to the roof to see if it would fly and it did! From that moment on they took it up to the roof every day, until my father got tired of going up the stairs and made a small opening in the door to the roof. From that day on, the pigeon flew up the stairway, through the hole in the door and returned the same way. Soon it sat on the handle of the door to the hallway to indicate it wanted to go outside.

The pigeon liked to stay close to my father and watch him play cards. Dad always had a cup of coffee next to him and the pigeon had got into the habit of drinking from it. That's where Mom drew the line. She told my father to cover his cup and gave the pigeon its own mug. Mom was used to letting it drink from the drippings of the fried steak which it liked very much. One day when it looked a bit sick, the vet came and said it was fine but it should cut down on the coffee and the fat. For the longest time we did not know whether this pigeon was a male or female so we called it pigeon in the way the French pronounce it, which sounds like "pee-jon." We found out it was a girl when it laid an egg in my father's lap! We also knew she was in love with him. She would only sit on his shoulder or lap and when we would point at a card he had overlooked, she would jump up and flap her wing against our hand. PeeJon died of old age; she must have been at least twelve years old.

One Day a Turkey Came Out for a Walk

One day a turkey came out for a walk
Along came a duck and they had a little talk
Gobble, gobble, gobble, Quack, quack, quack,
Goodbye, Goodbye, and they both went back.

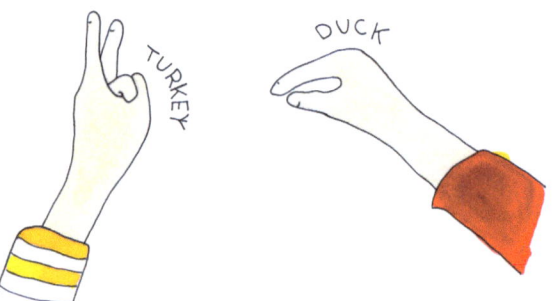

This rhyme is a hand and finger play and often turns into a funny situation when the duck changes into different animals that scare the poor turkey so much it runs away as fast as it can. The children love all the extensions, including the song by Bruce Hubbard.

Activity (Preschool and Kindergarten)
Everyone sits in a circle. Children hide both hands behind their back.

One day a turkey came out for a walk
(bring out one hand, make a fist, index and middle finger sticking out, and hold it in front of the face at eye level)

Along came a duck and they had a little talk
(show the other hand, fingers touching thumb to form a beak, facing the "turkey")

Gobble, gobble, gobble
(index and middle finger of the first hand move—turkey talks to the duck),

quack, quack, quack
(beak opens and closes—duck talks to the turkey)

Good bye,
(index and middle finger say goodbye)

Good bye,
(beak says goodbye)

And they both went back.
(both hands go behind the back)

Extensions

- Experiment with different emotional elements. For example, a sad or happy "goodbye."
- Keep the turkey but change the duck into other animals. The turkey goes for a walk again as in the original version and along comes, not a duck, but a different animal. Tell the children that when they choose another animal, they have to make its sound.
- Play the game with a row of turkeys and a row of ducks with one turkey and one duck standing inside the lines.

    A line of turkeys and ducks stand facing each other. One turkey and one duck are chosen to stand inside the lines. The lines of turkeys and ducks recite the first two lines of the verse, while the single turkey and duck imitate their respective animal. The last two lines are spoken by the single turkey and duck in turn except for "and they all went back" which is taken over by the "choir."
- Discuss the following sayings:

    Light as a feather... Free as a bird... Eating like a bird... Happy as a lark... Singing like a nightingale... Cozy as a bird's nest...
- Children choose one and act it out, by themselves or with partners while the others guess which saying they picked.
- Listen to Aaron Copland's *I bought Me a Cat* to hear baritone Bruce Hubbard sing and imitate animals with great flexibility and a beautiful voice. The form of the song is a "chain" where each new verse is followed by the ones that came before.

I bought me a cat, my cat pleased me,
I fed my cat under yonder tree,
My cat says fiddle eye fee.

I bought me a duck, my duck pleased me,
I fed my duck under yonder tree,
My duck says, "Quaa, quaa,"
My cat says fiddle eye fee.

I bought me a goose, my goose pleased me,
I fed my goose under yonder tree,
My goose says, "Quaw, quaw,"
My duck says...

I bought me a hen, my hen pleased me,
I fed my hen under yonder tree,
My hen says, "Shimmy shack, shimmy shack,"
My goose says...

I bought me a pig, my pig pleased me,
I fed my pig under yonder tree,
My pig says, "Griffey, griffey,"

My hen says...

I bought me a cow, my cow pleased me,
I fed my cow under yonder tree,
My cow says, "Moo, moo,"
My pig says...

I bought me a horse, my horse pleased me,
I fed my horse under yonder tree,
My horse says, "Neigh, neigh,"
My cow says...

I bought me a wife, my wife pleased me,
I fed my wife under yonder tree,
My wife says, "Honey, honey,"
My horse says...

The song is part of the album *For You, For Me: Songs of Copland, Gershwin, Sondheim, Berlin, Kern, Bernstein* played by The Orchestra of St. Lukes under the direction of Dennis Russell Davies. You can either buy the complete album or you can simply buy the MP3 version of the song which is track 5 on the album.

You will find them both on Amazon.com.

Once I Saw a Little Bird Go Hop, Hop, Hop

Once I saw a little bird go hop, hop, hop
And I said "Little bird will you stop, stop, stop?"
I went to the window to say, "How are you?"
But he shook his little tail and away he flew.

This delightful nursery rhyme asks for movement but it also likes to be recited with the help of body percussion or instruments.

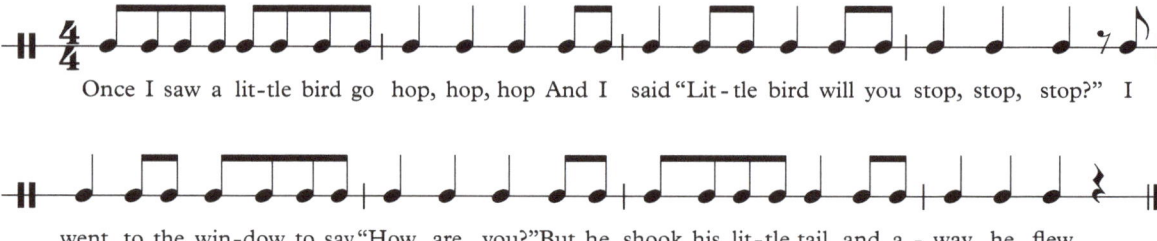

Activity 1 (Preschool, Kindergarten and First Grade)

Start the game with one couple standing inside a circle holding hands. At the end of the rhyme, both children choose a new partner. Continue, each time doubling the amount of children until all are playing.

Once I saw a little bird go hop, hop, hop
(hold hands and hop 3 times)

And I said little bird will you stop, stop, stop
(let go of your partner's hands, put your hands at your side and wag your finger at your partner, stamping on each "stop")

I went to the window to say, "How are you?"
(shake hands to the beat of the words)

But he shook his little tail and away he flew.
(shake bottom and "fly" away to get a new partner from the circle)

Louise, 5 years old

Activity 2 (Preschool, Kindergarten and First Grade)

This variation of the game invites the children to match the last words of each line of the verse to the sound of an instrument. This is not as difficult as one would think once they have the opportunity to know the sounds of a variety of instruments. To give them that opportunity, play the game of "Three Hoops and a Conductor." This game will not only familiarize them with the names of the instruments but give the teacher the opportunity to teach them how to play. The game offers the additional challenge of learning how to start and stop by following the visual cues of a conductor. I learned it during a training course from Susan Kennedy who is a very gifted and creative music and dance teacher.

Three Hoops and a Conductor

Playing cymbals and triangle

- Assemble instruments that can clearly be divided according to the material that produces their sound: metal, wood and skin. Demonstrate the proper way to play them.
- Put three hula hoops on the floor and place the instruments inside, according to type
- Ask what the reason is for the arrangement and name the individual instruments
- Invite the children to pick an instrument and sit close to the hoop it was picked from
- Allow them some time to play their instrument
- Explain that each group will play and stop according to the directions of a "conductor"
- Demonstrate the role of the conductor who directs the starting and stopping of each group by stepping in and out of the respective hoops. As long as the conductor is touching the inside of a hula hoop with any part of her body the children of that group must play continuously. As soon as she leaves the hoop, they stop.
- The conductor can jump from one hoop to the other, step in two hoops at once, stay inside for long or short periods or pretend to jump but instead land next to the hoop at the last second.

The teacher uses a cue to indicate another conductor and a change to another instrument.

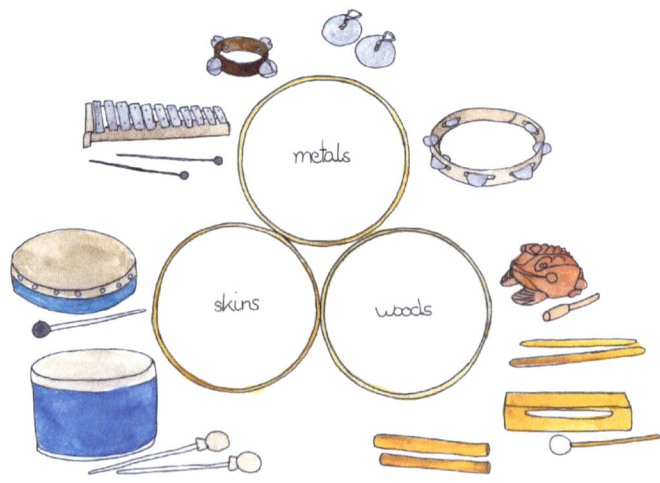

With the instruments inside the three hoops, use the variation of the rhyme in Activity 2 to play with the concept of "timbre" by finding out which instruments would best accentuate the words "hop" "stop" "How are you?" "away he flew."

Example

Once I saw a little bird go hop, hop, hop
(play hop, hop, hop, on a wood block after the words)

And I said little bird would you stop, stop, stop
(play stop, stop, stop, on a drum after the words)

I went to the window to say "How are you?"
(play "How are you?" on the wood block after the words)

But he shook his little tail and away he flew
(play the triangle after the words)

Activity 3 (Preschool, Kindergarten and First Grade)

Listen to *English Nightingale* from a selection of *The Flute's Garden of Delights* from Jacob Van Eyck (c. 1590–1657), played by Marion Verbruggen.

This beautiful piece is a great introduction into the world of instruments and the amazing talents of some of the world's best soloists. It is simple and short enough to be appreciated by young children.

"The Flute's Garden of Delight"

Jacob Van Eyck lived in the Netherlands and although blind from birth, he was the bell ringer for the Cathedral in Utrecht and director of all the bells, clocks and chimes of the city. He was also an excellent recorder player and his superiors appreciated his talents so much that they raised his salary on the condition that he play for the people strolling around on the church grounds.

Marion Verbruggen is one of the most extraordinary recorder virtuosos of our time and when you hear her "nightingale" you will have no doubt that she deserves this distinction.

English Nightingale

This piece is in AB AB AB form. A is a sweet melody announcing the coming of the nightingale and B, which is played in a different key, sings with the voice of the nightingale.

This first AB part takes one minute and it is possible to stop there at the break.

The second AB is a variation on the first. The A part announces the presence of a second bird and in the B part we can clearly distinguish two different nightingales. Every time the first one sings, the other one is answering. Again, there is a short break where you could stop.

The third AB which is again a variation of the original is a masterpiece of virtuosity, especially the B part. One gets so caught up in the cascades of delicate sounds that one forgets that there is actually a human being playing.

Even though three minutes might be long for some young listeners, it is worth trying.

You can buy the complete album or the MP3 version of the *English Nightingale*, which is track 8, on Amazon.com

Note

You must be familiar with the piece before presenting it to the children so you can point to some interesting details or ask questions like: "When do you first hear the nightingale sing?" or "Raise your hand when you hear the second nightingale."

1.4. HALLOWEEN RHYMES

Five Little Witches

Five little witches, flying through the air.
Up and down to see who's there.
Down came the rain and the thunder too.
Lightning struck and they all said "BOO!"

This classic example of a counting rhyme is excellent for playing with vocal and facial expressions and gestures. Using the expressive power of rhymes is a great tool for bringing text alive and helping children become aware of the sound of words. For example, it is natural to use not only a different gesture but also a different tone for "flying" compared to those used for the word "struck."

The extensions go a step further by encouraging the child to step into the shoes of another character.

Activity 1 (Preschool, Kindergarten and First Grade)

All sit or stand in a circle. Everyone says the rhyme using a "witche's voice" and performs the gestures with scary faces.

Five little witches, flying through the air
(one arm imitates flying)

Up and down to see who's there
(the same arm goes "up and down" and then the hand is placed on the forehead as if looking " to see who's there")

Down came the rain and the thunder too
(pat very fast, alternating left and right hands for "Down came the rain" and stamp fast with left and right feet on "and the thunder too")

Lightning struck,
(clap hard on "struck"),

and they all said BOO!
(whisper very slowly on "and they all said," pause after "said"... and then say a loud "BOO!")

Extensions

- Act out the rhyme
  Five children are in the middle of the circle, moving like witches or wizards. The rest of the class recites. When the rhyme is finished, the teacher chooses a clothing item to identify one of the five children and says: "One little wizard with a blue T shirt flew away and then there were……4, 3, 2, 1."

- A whole class of witches and wizards
  Five children form a choir and recite the rhyme. The rest of the class uses the entire room to act as witches and wizards. At the end of the rhyme all the witches and wizards drop to the floor.

Activity 2 (Kindergarten and First Grade)

Listen to: *The Garden Music of Insects, Frogs and Toads*, from *L'Enfant et les Sortilèges* (The Child and the Spells) by Maurice Ravel.

This piece, written for choir and orchestra, was inspired by a story the French author Colette wrote for her daughter. She was a great lover of art, music and dance and wrote beautifully about nature, especially her gardens and the woods where she grew up.

Both choir and orchestra imitate the sounds of different animals and create an impression of an enchanted and mysterious place. First we hear an owl and then a beautiful song bird; the choir adds other animals like insects, frogs and toads.

To play only the part you want the children to listen to, slowly fade to silence after 1:30 minutes of this 7:22 minute piece.

You can get the album or the MP3 version of the part you want to hear on Amazon.com. It is called *Ah! Quelle joie de to retrouver, Jardin!* (Ah! How much fun it is to find you again, Garden!) on track no. 6.

1.5. TRAIN RHYMES

One very cold winter I went with my family to Bavaria to spend Christmas with friends. We decided to travel by night on the Orient Express. After dinner we went to bed and fell asleep to the gentle rolling of our cabin. In the middle of the night we were awakened by the steward who told us the train had stopped because the conductor had decided it was unsafe to continue with so much snow on the tracks. He invited us for a cup of hot chocolate in the restaurant car and when we looked out the window we saw a dream landscape of hills and woods covered with snow and not a sound to be heard. We soon went back to sleep, thinking about the next morning when we would join the other travelers for a delicious breakfast of warm rolls, fresh butter, marmalade and bacon and eggs.

Engine, Engine, Number Nine

>Engine engine number nine
>Going down Chicago line
>If the engine jumps the track
>Will I get my money back?

This nursery rhyme involves a lively and entertaining movement activity and is always received with great enthusiasm because trains are very popular with young children. As an extra bonus the children get an experience of two mathematical processes.

Before You Begin

Talk about the conductor, the caboose, the whistle, buying a train ticket and whatever else they want to say about trains. Bring a whistle, a hat and a bag for the conductor and pennies for the children to buy a ticket.

Activity 1 (Preschool and Kindergarten)

At the beginning of the activity, everyone is sitting in a circle.

Give each child a penny to pay for a train ticket and choose a conductor who will have a bag hanging on her shoulder to collect the pennies. The teacher blows the whistle and the game starts.

The children recite the rhyme while the conductor moves around the circle to the beat. She stops at the end of the rhyme and taps the head of the child next to her.

This child gets up, drops her penny in the bag and holds on to the conductor's shirt or shoulder with both hands.

The other children close the gap left by the child on the train. That way, every time a child leaves, the circle gets smaller while the "train" gets longer. This gives the children a visual representation of two abstract concepts: the shrinking circumference of a circle and the growing length of a line.

Play the game until all the children are on the train. The last one is the caboose!

Note

Even though the children would love to blow that whistle, they understand about germs.

Activity 2 (Preschool and Kindergarten)

In this second activity, which makes for a more special train ride, the teacher plays the drum, maracas, wood block, slide whistle, tambourine and chimes. Adapt your choice of instruments to your circumstances or preferences.

Give each child a penny to pay for a ticket and choose a conductor. Blow the whistle and start the game.

At the end of the game, when everyone is onboard, the train will take them to some very special countries. When the rhyme stops, the teacher announces each new location.

"First stop: BUNNY COUNTRY!"

The children get off the train by letting go of each other's shirt or shoulders and hop around like bunnies while the teacher plays the beat on the drum.

Everyone gets back on the train at the sound of the whistle.

"Next stop: SNAKE COUNTRY!"

The teacher plays the maracas and everyone slithers around on the floor, hissing like snakes.

"Next stop: RUNNING COUNTRY!"

Use the wood block to play a fast beat.

"Next stop: UP AND DOWN COUNTRY!"

Use the slide whistle while the children go from standing very tall to crouching down or somewhere in between when the slide whistle gets "stuck." Experiment with different speeds.

"Next stop: HOW DO YOU DO COUNTRY!"

The children walk around shaking hands while saying: "How do you do?"

"Next stop: ONE LEGGED COUNTRY!"

Use drum, rhythm stick, tambourine or wood block while the children hop on one leg.

"Next stop: BUTTERFLY COUNTRY!"

Use chimes for free movement.

Suggested Children's Books
Peet, Bill. *The Caboose Who Got Loose*. Boston: Houghton Miffin, 1971.
Lenski, Lois. *The Little Train*. New York: Random House. 1940

1.6. FOOD RHYMES

On the first Sunday of every November, it was the custom in Belgium to invite the family over for waffles. Early in the morning, the housewives made the dough and placed it next to the stove to let it rise. This process took several hours and there was always a lot of screaming when somebody forgot to close a door and the cold air threatened to make the dough "fall." When everything went well, and the pot showed signs of overflowing, the bake began. We ate our waffles as soon as they came out of the iron, hot and crisp and covered them with butter and sugar. Today, waffles can be eaten at any time of the year at a tea room. Now there are more toppings to choose from and my favorite is a big dollop of whipped cream as you can see in the picture.

Belgian waffle and pancakes

Pat-a-Cake

Pat a cake, pat a cake baker's man
Bake me a cake as fast as you can
Pat it and roll it and mark it with a B
Put it in the oven for baby and me.

We play this well known nursery rhyme in groups that double with each repetition until the whole class is playing as one group. This is another example of an activity where the vehicles for learning are only the voice and movement.

Pat a cake, pat a cake bak-er's man Bake me a cake as fast as you can

Pat it and roll it and mark it with a B Put it in the ov-en for ba-by and me.

Activity 1 (Preschool and Kindergarten)

Pat a cake, pat a cake baker's man, bake me a cake as fast as you can
(clap to the beat)

Pat it and roll it and mark it with a B
(pat one hand with the other, roll your hands around each other and trace the letter B with your pointer on the palm of your hand)

put it in the oven
(cup both hands)

for baby and me.
(cradle arms as if cuddling a baby and rock)

Activity 2 (Preschool and Kindergarten)

Choose a partner and repeat the activity. With a little help from the teacher the children keep doubling their number after every repetition until the whole class forms one group.

Movement

- With a partner: face partner, forearms raised, palms of hands facing partner. Clap partner's hands on the first line. Do the patting, rolling, marking and putting in the oven individually. Hold hands and swing your partner's arms from left to right on "for baby and me."
- In groups of four/eight, etc. Stand in a circle and raise your forearms sideways, palms facing friends on the left and the right to do the clapping. Do the patting, rolling, marking and putting in the oven individually. Hold hands and swing arms forward and backward on "for baby and me."

Sideways clappingClapping sideways in a circle

- Keep doubling the amount of children until all form one group.

Mix a Pancake

Mix a pancake, stir a pancake, pour a pancake in the pan
Fry a pancake, toss a pancake, catch a pancake if you can

Use this nursery rhyme with the appropriate gestures for all grades. Add a speech ostinato[1] for an additional challenge in Kindergarten and First Grade.

Before you begin
Talk about the different actions (italicized below) used to make pancakes. Can they show the appropriate gesture for each one? Every time a gesture is shown, the whole class repeats it.

Activity 1 (Preschool, Kindergarten and First Grade)
Mix a pancake, *stir* a pancake, *pour* a pancake **in the pan.**
Fry a pancake, *toss* a pancake, *catch* a pancake **if you can.**

Recite the rhyme with the appropriate gestures for the actions and add three claps at the end of each line for the last 3 words.

Activity 2 (Kindergarten and First Grade)
Make the activity a bit more challenging by adding another layer to the rhyme like the following short sentence:

Butter them, *sugar* them, *serve* them hot (clap)

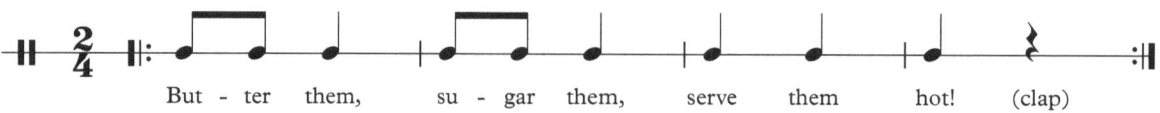

Recite the new sentence and ask the children to use the appropriate gestures for *butter, sugar* and *serve*.

---

1 An ostinato is a musical phrase that is repeated continuously without change.

Divide the class into two groups:

> Group one recites Mix a Pancake and plays unpitched percussion instruments (rhythm sticks, drum, claves, etc.) on the italic and bold words.
> Group two recites the new sentence with the appropriate gestures and a clap at the end.

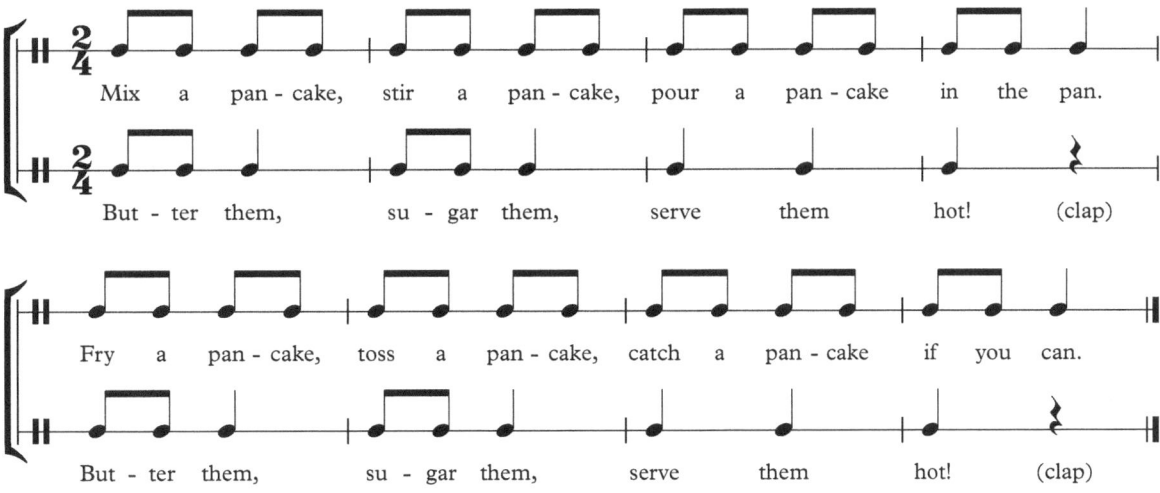

Extension

Eating Belgian pancakes

In Belgium, pancakes are still considered a special treat and are served whenever you want to spoil your family and friends. They are larger and thinner than American pancakes and eaten with butter, brown sugar and a squeeze of orange juice, as you see in the picture on page 28.

Make one "Belgian" pancake for each child in the class. Put butter, brown sugar and a generous squeeze of fresh orange juice on them and roll them up like a cigar so they can eat them with their hands. The melted butter and orange juice mix with the sugar and are mostly absorbed into the pancake so you have a nice, not too sweet taste and a pancake that will not drip. Bring them to school and explain why these are not the same as American pancakes. Expect to hear from their Moms that these are the best pancakes ever!

Recipe for Belgian Pancakes

Ingredients:
⅔ cup of unbleached self rising wheat flour (or ⅔ cup of unbleached white flour and 1 tsp of baking powder), 2 large eggs, pinch of salt, 1 cup of whole milk, a few drops of vanilla extract and 1 Tbs of canola oil.

To prepare the dough:
Combine the flour, eggs, ¼ of the milk and the vanilla extract in a bowl and whisk until smooth. The mixture should be fairly thick. Add the rest of the milk, a tablespoon of oil and mix again until smooth.

Grease a 10" skillet and place over medium heat. When the pan is hot, add 3 tablespoons of the batter and lift the pan quickly so the batter coats the entire bottom of the pan. When the top of the pancake is almost dry, turn it with a spatula. When the other side is brown, slide the pancake onto a warm plate. Cooking time on one side will be about 45 seconds and 20 seconds on the second side. Serve them with butter and brown sugar and a squeeze of orange juice.

Pancakes are best made right before eating them. The way it happened in my family is that when the dough was ready and the table set, Mom started baking and slid a cake on someone's plate as soon as it was done. She made sure everyone had a lot of turns and there has never been a bake where I wished I could have eaten more.

Belgian pancakes with brown sugar, butter and orange juice

What's Your Favorite Food?

In the following activities we use words for food or drink to familiarize the children with rhythmic units that are the building blocks of most of the children's rhymes and songs that appear in this book. They are the material the children will use for further musical exploration through speech, body percussion, movement and instrumental play. To fix them even more firmly in mind we will also use them for our first encounter with rhythmic notation.

Activity 1 (Preschool, Kindergarten and First Grade)

Everyone sitting in a circle: teacher starts by saying their favorite food then invites the child next to them to do the same. One by one, the children take a turn and each time a new word is added, everyone repeats the series from the beginning ending on the new word. For example:
   1) apple sauce
   2) apple sauce, lollypop
   3) apple sauce, lollypop, chicken nuggets
   4) apple sauce, lollypop, chicken nuggets, lemonade

Extension
   Add a gesture to each word to show how the food is consumed.

Activity 2 (Preschool, Kindergarten and First Grade)

The teacher speaks and plays the name of her favorite food on a floor drum; children repeat and clap the word. She then slides the drum to the person next to her. Each time someone has spoken and played the name of their favorite food, all the other children in the group repeat it and clap it.

Note

A floor drum works better than a hand drum because it's more natural for young children to hold a mallet and strike something. Show how to tap the drum in the middle with the "head" of the mallet softly so as not to damage the "skin" of the drum. I ask the children to sit on their knees with their bottom touching their heels and pass the drum to their neighbor when they are finished.

Activity 3 (Preschool, Kindergarten and First Grade)

The following rhyme which uses several rhythmic building blocks from the foregoing activity was inspired by track no. 30 on the CD "Yesterdays" from The San Francisco School Orff Ensemble 2011. This CD features music played by the children at the school and was created by Doug Goodkin, James Harding and Sofia Lopez who have made a CD each year to showcase their work at The San Francisco School.

I Like Choc'late Sauce

I like choc'late sauce, I like pie
I like choc'late sauce and lots and lots of pie.
Choc'late sauce, lots of pie, go together like you and I
Choc'late sauce, lots of pie, we're together you and I
Stamp your feet, slap your knees, turn around and FREEZE!

Stand up, recite rhyme, perform body percussion and freeze in a shape on "FREEZE!"

Variation: children repeat rhyme as they walk hand in hand with a partner in any direction they want, stop on "lots and lots of pie" and then perform the rest of the rhyme as before, clapping their partner's hands.

Guess the Food Word Played on the Drum

This is a continuation of "What's Your Favorite Food"? It is based on speech play and rather challenging but Kindergarten and First Grade children can do it. With a visual representation of the rhythms of the words, we are going to take our first step toward music notation.

Activity (Kindergarten and First Grade)

Repeat Activities 1 and 2 from "What's Your Favorite Food?"

Work with the children to categorize the food words they have chosen according to their rhythm. Ask: "Which food words have the same rhythm (sound the same) when we play them on the drum?"

Form five groups (or less) of children sitting together with those whose word has the same rhythm as theirs.

Avoid words that start with a weak beat (upbeat) like vanilla, potatoes, sardines, etc. The children need not be aware of the reason why.

Examples:

One syllable: juice, jam, bread, fudge

Two syllables: pan-cake, piz-za, ice cream, car-rot,

Three syllables: chick-en-soup, broc-co-li, choc'late sauce, lem-on pie

Three syllables: red pep-per, crab ap-ple

Four syllables: buck-wheat noo-dles, ma-ca-ro-ni, mashed po-ta-toes

Note

Three syllable words can be pronounced in two ways producing two different rhythms.

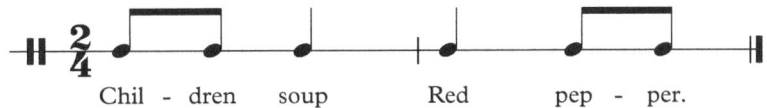

Pre-notation

Ask each one of the five groups to agree on one word. The examples I have chosen are bread, pan-cake, lem-on pie, red pep-per, ma-ca-ro-ni.

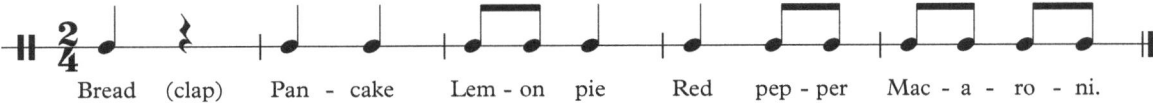

Create a visual representation of the rhythm of each group's word, using plastic cups of two different sizes and a napkin. Such concrete representations are a first step towards the abstract conceptualization required for note reading. Place the corresponding cups in front of each group.

- Use the five examples of cup formations and the words they represent to play "Guess which food word is played on the drum?"

The teacher plays one of the rhythms on the drum and children guess the corresponding word. Then a student plays one of the four rhythms for the others to guess.

Extend further with sequences of two words (more difficult).

I.7. A COMPLETE MUSIC AND MOVEMENT PROJECT BASED ON CATS AND MICE

Ideally, a curriculum based on one theme should be done as a collaborative effort with all the teachers at the school. Many different aspects of a theme could be researched and connections between the subjects could be explored. It would also be rewarding for the music teacher who often feels more like a visitor than a member of a team. I know of schools where this is done with impressive results.

Five Little Mice

Five little mice came out to play
Gathering crumbs along the way
Out came pussycat sleek and black
Four little mice went scattering back.

Cats and Mice Project Part 1

We perform this delightful nursery rhyme with finger play. The children love it, especially when the music teacher performs her silly part at the end. Use it as a song or a rhyme.

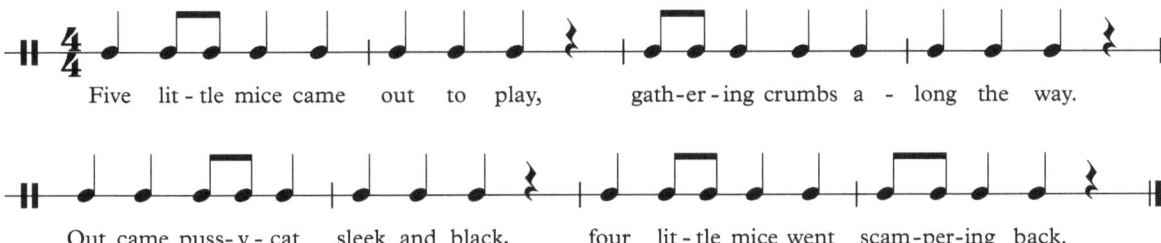

Activity (Preschool and Kindergarten)

Everyone sits in a circle: we use the fingers of one hand as the five mice, while the other hand pretends to be the cat. Both hands are out of sight as each new verse starts. During the course of the rhyme, the "mice" disappear one by one until only one is left at which point the game changes slightly because that mouse is smarter than the others.

Five little mice came out to play
(one hand with fingers stretched and spread out comes from behind the back and mimics the mice playing).

Gathering crumbs along the way
(the five fingers pretend to eat crumbs off the floor)

Out came pussycat, sleek and black

(the other hand comes out, fingers touching thumb like a mouth that opens and closes. The mouth comes closer and closer to a mouse and, as soon as the words are spoken, grabs one finger)

Four little mice went scampering back
(both hands return behind the back)

The cat eats one mouse after another until only one is left. The children have decided though that the cat should not eat the last mouse because he is too smart. Everyone finds a place underneath their clothes where they will hide it as soon as the cat appears.

One little mouse came out to play
(one "mouse" comes out)

Gathering crumbs along the way
(the "mouse" first eats some crumbs off the floor and then quickly hides, before the cat arrives)

Out came pussycat sleek and black
(the cat arrives and looks around, surprised to see there is no mouse. After a while she has to return without one)

One little mouse went scampering back
(the mouse comes happily out of her hiding place)

Note

I usually add a silly joke to the part when the cat comes out and is surprised not to find a mouse. I pretend she mistakes first my nose and then my ear for a mouse and bites them. The surprise makes me cry out and jump up and is now an eagerly awaited moment in the game.

Nicole Hammer

I. Rhymes

Pussycat, Pussycat, What do you Want?

Cats and Mice Project: Part 2

A Guessing Game

From the answer to their question "Pussycat, Pussycat, what do you want?" the children have to guess who's voice they are hearing. Guessing games are very popular and have been around for a long time as you see in this detail of Bruegel's "Children's Games" where two boys are sitting on another boy's back who is leaning on a fourth one. Only if he guesses how many fingers one of the boys is holding up will he be relieved.

Bruegel, Pieter the Elder. Detail from Children's Games. 1560.
Licensed by Art Resources, NY

Activity (Preschool, Kindergarten and First Grade)

Everyone sits in a circle. One child sits on a chair in the center of the circle and closes her eyes or is blindfolded. Another child, the "Pussycat," quietly steps behind her and taps her on the shoulder.

The child in the chair asks: "Pussycat, Pussycat, what do you want?"

The cat answers: "Milk."

The blindfolded child guesses the name of the "Pussycat" from the sound of her voice.

If she's wrong she remains in the chair, if she's right the pussycat takes her place and a new cat is chosen.

Note

Very young children often do not like to wear a blindfold and prefer to close their eyes instead.

His Majesty's Cat

Cats and Mice Project: Part 3

This excellent language game from Music for Children Volume 1[1] encourages children to use words in an expressive way, with facial expressions, gestures and body postures.

Activity (Preschool, Kindergarten and First Grade)

Everyone sits in a circle, and thinks about the kind of cat His Majesty might have. The children then take turns to announce their idea.

Examples: "His Majesty's cat is a lazy/wild/cute/sleepy/snoring/sad/shy/mean/angry/nervous/happy/unhappy/hungry/hot/cold/musical cat."

Each time someone voices a description, the group echoes it.

Extension

Children use facial expressions, movement and voice to emphasize a descriptive word and the other children echo.

Repeat without the voice and have the other children guess.

Note

We need to take advantage of a time in their life when most children are not self-conscious to give them a taste of the freedom involved in the ability to express one's feelings. The safe environment of the classroom and the example of some of their friends with less apprehension often gives the very shy among them courage to get into the game.

---

1 A basic work in the Orff-Schulwerk canon with contributions and articles from several music teachers, co-ordinated by Hermann Regner from The Orff-Institute, Salzburg. American Edition Schott Music Corp. 1982

The Mouse's Husband

Cats and Mice Project: Part 4

This story from Japan of the mouse's husband is ideal for a play because the same scene is repeated several times. The text given here is only a suggestion; you may want to change it to suit your students. The children also have the choice of following the text or choosing their own words. The role of the narrator is played by the teacher or an older child. In Kindergarten and First Grade, we performed it with self-made puppets.

Activity (Kindergarten and First Grade)

Tell the story of the mouse's husband

Two mice, a father and a mother, decide that only the Most Powerful Being in the Universe will do for a husband for their daughter. They make a big ladder and climb all the way up to visit the sun, but the sun points to the cloud as being the most powerful, because clouds often hide the sun who can't do anything about it. The cloud also denies being the mightiest and points instead to the wind which moves clouds here and there at will. The wind in turn points to the wall as the strongest power, since the wall will not move however strongly the wind blows against it. When the mice arrive back on earth, the wall shows them the reason why they needn't look any further: a mouse has made a hole in the wall and moved inside! The mice find out that they themselves are the most powerful! The story ends with the daughter marrying a nice mouse whom she liked already anyway.

Play

Narrator: Once upon a time there was a family of mice: a mother, a father, and their beautiful daughter. When she was old enough to get married, the parents decided that only the Most Powerful Being in the Universe was good enough to be her husband. As soon as they agreed that the sun was the most powerful, the mice built a very big ladder and went up and up and up until they reached the sun. Once they were up there, father mouse said:

Father: Sun, sun, you are the Most Powerful Being in the Universe. Please marry my daughter.

Sun: OOOOH! I would love to marry her but I can't.

Father: Why not?

Sun: I am not the most powerful. The cloud is more powerful than me. The cloud comes in front of me and hides me.

Narrator: So the mice went looking for the cloud and when they found one, the mother mouse said:

Mother: Cloud, cloud, you are the Most Powerful Being in the Universe. Please marry my daughter?

Cloud: OOOOOH! I would love to marry her but I can't.

Mother: Why not?

Cloud: I am not the most powerful. The wind is more powerful than me. The wind loves to blow me away.

Narrator:	So the mice went looking for the wind. They could not see it of course but when they heard it the daughter said:
Daughter:	Wind, wind, you are the Most Powerful Being in the Universe. Please marry me?
Wind:	OOOOH! I would love to marry you, but I can't
Daughter:	Why not?
Wind:	I am not the most powerful. The wall is more powerful than me. I blow very hard and the wall does not move.
Narrator:	So the mice went back down to earth and looked for the wall. Soon they saw a very big one and together the mother and father said:
Mother and Father:	Wall, wall, you are the Most Powerful Being in the Universe. Please marry our daughter?
Wall:	OOOOH! I would love to marry her but I can't.
Mother and Father:	Why not?
Wall:	Because I am not the most powerful being. The mice are more powerful than me. With their sharp teeth they make holes and then they build their house inside me.
Narrator:	The mice were very happy to know that they were the Most Powerful Beings in the Universe and they arranged for their daughter to marry Tom, a handsome mouse who loved her already. They married and had a really big party. They ate lots of yummy cheese and they played and danced to their favorite song: PUSSY CAME PARADING.

Puppets and props

One way to create the "puppets" for this play is to have the children make drawings of the different characters, color them, cut them out and glue them on lollypop sticks. Another is to find samples yourself and ask the children to color them and add details to the mouse designs to show the difference between Mom, Dad, Daughter and Tom. Music teachers usually don't have the time to spend on art projects but classroom teachers can take this as far as they want and experiment with different materials.

Pussy Came Parading

Pussy came parading out of a barn
With a pair of bagpipes under her arm
She sang hurray and fiddle-dee-dee
The mouse has married the bumblebee
Pipe, cat, dance, mouse
We're having a wedding at our little house

Cats and Mice Project: Part 5

As soon as I read the text of this lovely old English nursery rhyme a song jumped into my head. I turned it into a dance because it was asking for it and included a body percussion pattern that I remembered from a dance in a Jane Austen movie.

Nicole Hammer

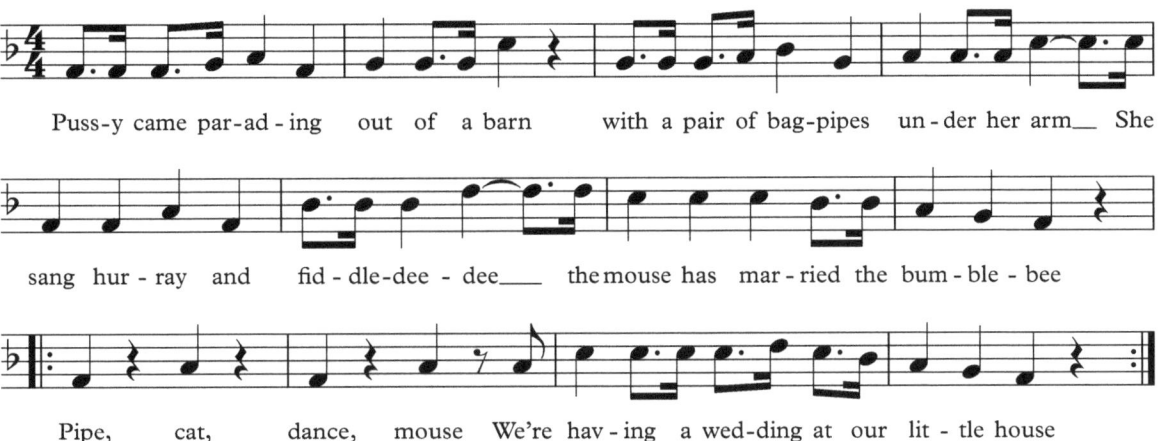

Activity (Preschool, Kindergarten and First Grade)

Teacher and children sit in a circle, one couple stands inside, side by side, holding hands. Together they perform the dance and the percussion pattern. When they are finished, they separate and choose a new partner, each time doubling the amount of children until everyone is dancing.

Pussy came parading out of a barn, with a pair of bagpipes under her arm.
She sang hurray and fiddle-dee-dee, the mouse has married the bumblebee
(One couple inside the circle joins hands and walks around to the beat of the song. They stop at "bumblebee," let go of their hands and face each other)

Pipe, cat, dance, mouse
(They perform the body percussion and clap each other's hands at the end).

We're having a wedding at our little house
(They do a full two-hand turn.)

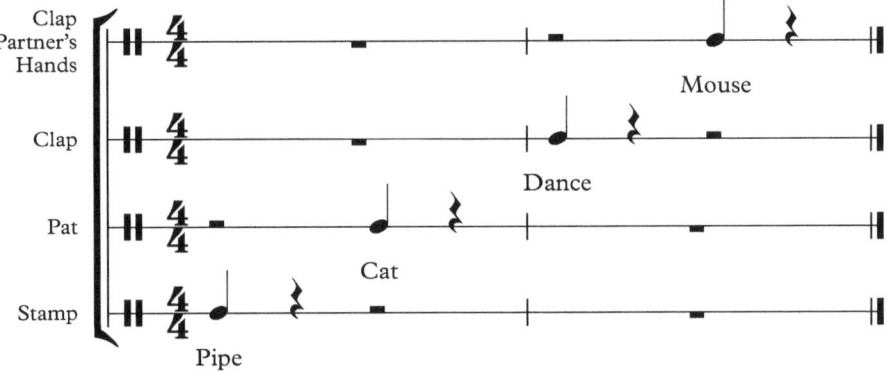

Listening to "Cat Music"

(Cats and mice project: Part 6)

Listen to *Duetto buffo di due gatti* (Humorous duet for two cats), sung by the beautiful voices of Felicity Lott and Ann Murray.

The "lyrics" of the duet consist entirely of the repeated word "Meow".

Get the complete album *Sweet Power of Song*, directed by Graham Johnson, or the cat duet as an MP3 version. You will find both on Amazon.com.

Art Project

Cats and mice project: Part 7

The arts teacher Sandy Reid (http://artwithsandy.wix.com/sandysartstudio) used the story of "The Mouse's Husband" to create an activity for her students based on the Japanese ink brush technique called Sumi.

II. MOVEMENT AND LISTENING GAMES

A note about movement in Preschool, Kindergarten and First Grade.

Movement combined with music and language should be a part of the daily program in Pre-school, Kindergarten and First Grade.

Through play, children should experience basic types of movement such as walking, running, skipping, bouncing, jumping, swaying and turning as well as the following concepts:

- up and down, front and back, under, over, on, beside, through, high and low
- loud and soft, heavy and light, round and straight
- circle, pair, group, line
- together, apart, simultaneously, one after the other

They should practice movement combination such as:

- walking and clapping, walking and playing an instrument, skipping and waving a scarf

They should learn to perform different types of movement in succession

- walking, running, skipping and crawling to the sound of the drum for example

They should learn how to:

- form a circle that goes clockwise(CW), counter clock wise(CCW), to the centre and back
- form pairs, with or without holding hands
- form groups of four and eight
- find a partner after a free movement
- stand in line behind a leader, change leader
- dance to rhymes, songs and recorded music

The daily program should include free individual play as well as group movement play.

In free movement play, the children can experiment with their unique physical capacities and work on their coordination, spatial awareness and kinesthetic sense.

In group movement play they learn to adapt to others, follow a common tempo and certain rules imposed by the dance.

Red Rover

I grew up in a quiet city street at a time when there were hardly any cars. When we weren't in school, we were outside playing ball games, hopscotch, leap frog, and a game very much like Red Rover where we would all stand across the street and the one who was IT, stood on the opposite side with his face turned to the wall. He would say: "Een, twee, drie, piano!" while everyone tried to sneak up and tag him.

A lot of the games we played can be seen in the painting "Kinderspelen" (Children's Games) by the Flemish artist Pieter Bruegel the Elder, who was born a long time ago in my neck of the woods.

Bruegel, Pieter the Elder (c. 1525–1569). Children's Games. 1560. Licensed by Art Resource, NY

Activity (Preschool, Kindergarten and First Grade)
When you play this game with very young children, it's best to be Red Rover yourself.

Red Rover asks the children to sit on one side of the room. On the other side is their home. They are allowed to cross and go home only when they execute the commands of Red Rover.

Red Rover calls them one by one saying:" Red Rover, Red Rover, let Jason HOP ON ONE LEG OVER." If Jason does not succeed he has to go back.

Other simple commands are: walk, tip-toe, hop, skip, and skate, walk sideways, backward, jump backward, gallop like a horse, jump like a frog.

More adventurous ones: walking while pretending to have a cast or carrying a very heavy object.

More complicated commands: walk with four big steps and hop with four little hops, or, turn around three times and hop on one leg three times.

Red rover can also invite several people at once, like: anyone wearing black shoes, a white T-shirt, green shorts, etc.

Extension
Use a large reproduction of "Children's Games" and explore the painting
- Create a set of cards with copies of details and use them to recreate some of the scenes.
- Each group or individual presents their scene in front of the whole class and they guess where it fits in the painting.
- Bring costumes, dolls, masks, and any prop that can help fire the imagination.
- Take pictures!
- Use the cards to create stories with the different characters

Examples

1. Playing dress-up and staging a wedding
2. Mounting a hobby horse
3. Blind man's bluff
4. Staging a baptism
5. Playing pipe and drum

Walk to the Drum

In this game, the children need to listen carefully to the teacher's commands which challenge their control of movement and listening skills.

Activity (Preschool, Kindergarten and First Grade)

This activity is based on a series of beats played by the teacher on a drum. The children walk around the room and follow the teacher's commands:

    WALK around the room at the sound of the drum and STOP when the drum stops.
    Walk BACKWARDS, SIDEWAYS, and STOP when the drum stops
    Walk around the room, STOP when the drum stops and make a SHAPE
    Walk with a PARTNER, STOP when the drum stops. Make a SHAPE with your partner.
    Walk backwards and sideways with your PARTNER, etc.

Move to the Sound of the Instruments

Use the different tone colors of the wood block, maracas, drum and cymbals as a motivator for movement and add a story to stimulate the children's imagination. For the example below I created a "Pinocchio" story, but you can, of course, come up with your own narrative. This is a fun game that encourages listening, imagination, creativity and control of movement and helps the children understand the meaning of tone color (timbre), the unique sound of an instrument. In this game, each instrument's tone color evokes different reactions.

Activity (Preschool, Kindergarten and First Grade)

The children are spread out across the room, and move to the sound of different instruments the narrator (teacher) is playing. When the instrument stops, they freeze. The narrator needs to put a lot of expression in her voice, going from sad to hopeful and excited, happy and content.

Narrator: Once upon a time there was a classroom full of wooden marionettes that walked around with stiff bodies, legs and arms, taking very small steps. Whenever they could, they would go for a walk to see how the real boys and girls were moving because they wanted so much to be like them. But they always had to come back home just the same as they were before.

Teacher plays WOOD BLOCK and the children start to move.

Narrator: One day, while they were walking around, something strange happened to them. Their bodies started to tickle all over. Their arms and legs started to wiggle. They could shake their heads and their bottoms, bend their arms and legs and move their toes and fingers.

Teacher plays MARACAS or TAMBOURINE and the children start wiggling and shaking.

Narrator: They soon realized they had become real boys and girls. Now they could run or skip or jump, they could even skip with their friends and hold their hands.

Teacher plays a skipping beat on the DRUM and the children start to move.

Narrator: They were so happy that they did not notice it was getting dark, and suddenly they began to feel very tired. They slowly walked home, stretched their bodies as wide as they could, yawned and went to sleep, dreaming about the next day and all the new games they were going to play.

Teacher plays CYMBAL.

Moving with Objects

I Let a Song Go Out of My Heart

As a young man in the nineteen thirties, Dad had fallen madly in love with American swing. His collection of jazz records was destroyed during the bombings of WWII but as soon as the blockades were lifted he ordered every jazz record he could get. We listened to Lionel Hampton, Benny Goodman, Duke Ellington, Harry James, Louis Armstrong, Count Basie, Charlie Parker and Glenn Miller to name just a few. Dad was always drumming on something, and finally bought a drum set because of his hero Gene Krupa.

In the following game, we use bean bags to develop control of movement and balance. Play the game with Duke Ellington's masterpiece, *I Let a Song Go Out of My Heart* from *The Essential Duke Ellington* on Amazon.com.

Activity (Preschool, Kindergarten, First Grade)

- Walk or move slowly while balancing a beanbag on head, shoulders, hands or elbows. Sit down at the end of the song.
- Choose a partner, move slowly to the music holding the bag between elbows, hips, forehead or shoulders.

Note
The smooth, sensual, swinging sounds of the saxophones in this beautiful piece are the ideal stimulus for the controlled but fluid movements that are the prerequisite for success in this game.

Balancing bean bags

III. SONGS

Singing was an important part of growing up during my childhood. Mothers and grandmothers sang to their children from the day they were born. They had a large repertoire of their own, mostly sentimental ballads about the trials and tribulations of relationships and arias from famous Italian or French operas. Mom and Grandma sang the opera tunes in the original language while Dad preferred the more saucy versions in our Ghent dialect. They knew songs that commemorated important events, like the landing of the first airplane acrobat in a field close to our house. It seemed as if a song appeared as soon as something unusual had happened. We children knew all those songs and although we didn't always understand the words, we quickly figured out the difference between the ones we could sing aloud and those we better kept to ourselves. We had our own songs which we learned from each other and they came to us at the same time as the games they were made for: ball games, jumping rope games, counting-out games to determine who was to be "It" and songs for rainy days when we played indoors. "Up and Down, Up and Down" is a very old rainy-day game with a tower and a dragon as the subject which is not surprising when one looks at this picture taken from the center of Ghent. The tower in the front is a Belfry or fortified tower. It has a huge gilded dragon on the top that was cast in 1377. The people of Ghent are very proud of their belfry because it is the highest in existence. It used to contain a famous bell called "Roland "who's sound was heard whenever there was danger, storm or fire or when victory was won.

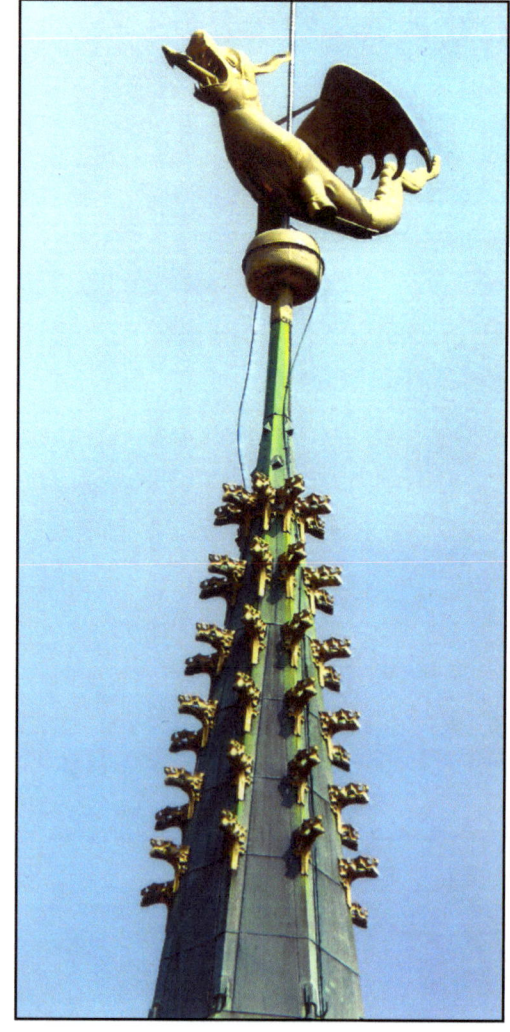

Up and Down, Up and Down

Song and game

Preparation:
Players sit around a table. The first player puts a fist on the table, thumb sticking up. The next player grabs first player's thumb with one hand and sticks his thumb up as well, which is grabbed by the next person and so on. Then everyone adds their other hand and the tower gets higher and higher. The last person keeps his thumb up to represent the dragon on the tower.

Activity:
When the song starts, all hands go up and down to the rhythm without breaking the tower. At the end of the song everyone hides their hands and teeth.

Nicole Hammer

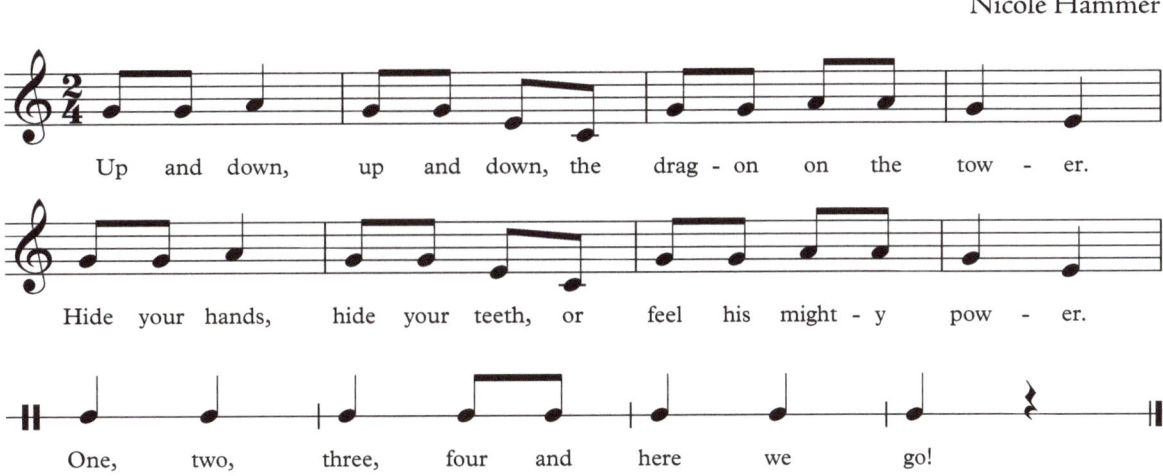

The first player to show a hand or a glimpse of teeth gets a punishment that is decided upon by everyone. The challenge is to make your friends laugh hard enough so they open their mouth or show their hands while making sure you don't.

Pop Up Game

Chant with movement

Formation: circle

Activity

The children crouch down, pretending to be a slice of toast inside a toaster. The teacher starts the game, chanting:

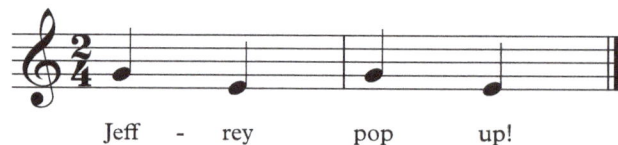

Jeffrey sits upright and calls another child:

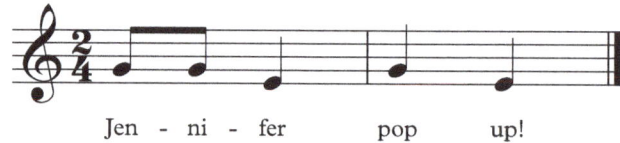

The game continues until everyone has popped out of the toaster.

Note

The short melodic motif (chant) used in this game is an introduction to pitch matching.

Noor "in the toaster"

Who Has the Walnut?

Chant with objects

Formation: circle

Preparation
Fill a bag with as many objects as there are children playing the game.

Activity
Take the objects out, place them in the middle of the circle and ask the children to name and remember them.

Return the objects to the bag and go around the circle. The children take one object and hide it behind their back.

The teacher starts the game with this chant:

Who has the wal - nut?

The child who has the walnut places it in front of her and sings "I have the walnut" using the same pitch.

Then the child continues and sings: "Who has the ...", and the game continues until all the objects have been named and are in front of the children.

Extension
+ Use letters or numbers.
+ Use geometric shapes.

Examples

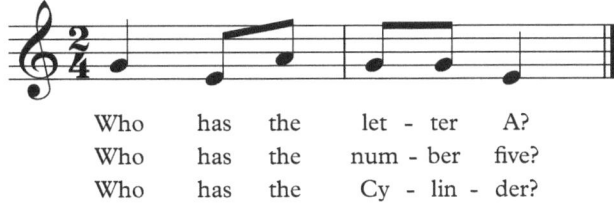

Who has the let - ter A?
Who has the num - ber five?
Who has the Cy - lin - der?

NOOR'S "SHEIPS"

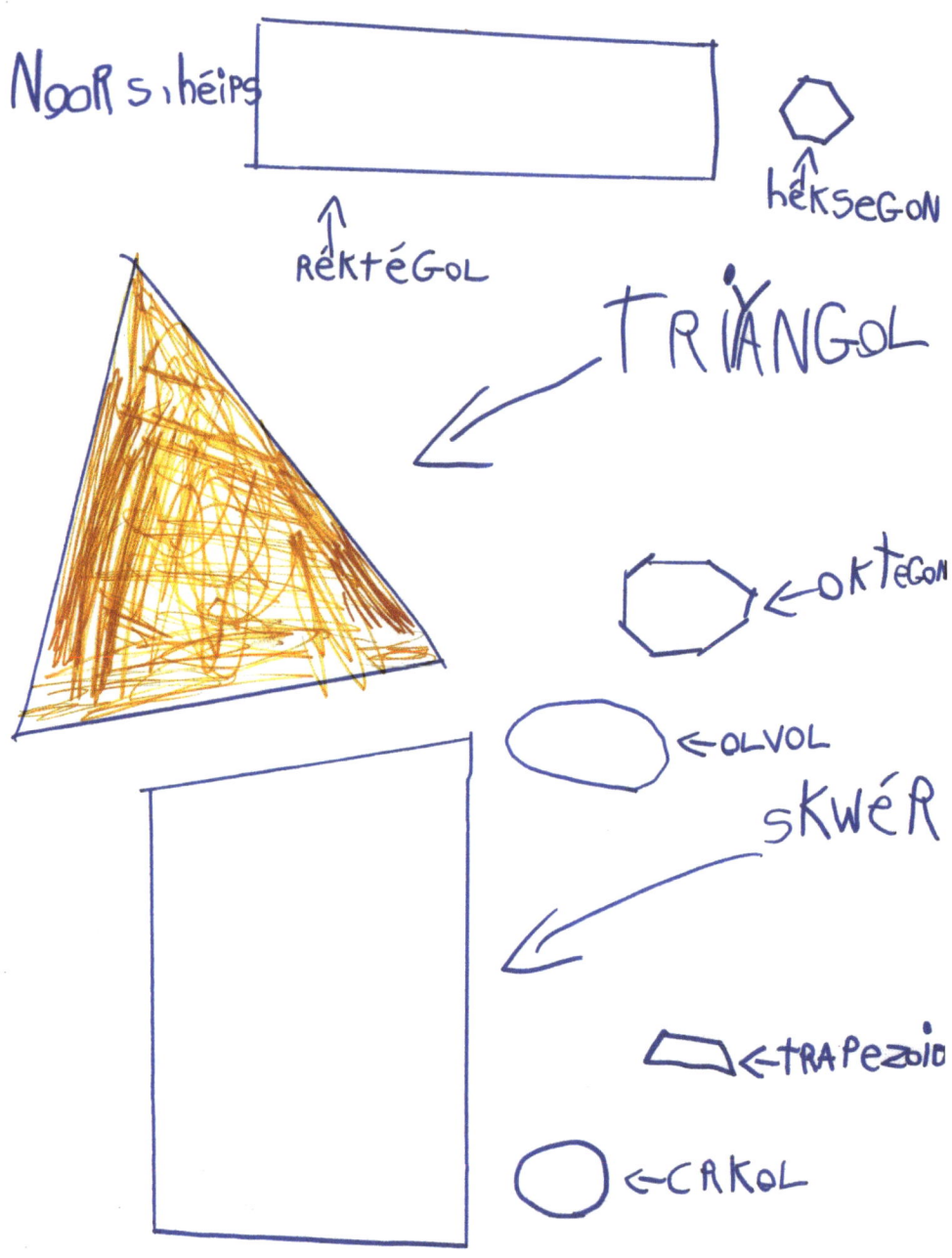

Noor, 8 years old

When Noor heard about the game with the geometric shapes she sent me this drawing. She is homeschooled and raised by a French-speaking dad and an English/Dutch-speaking mom and started writing in French and English with very interesting results. When she was first asked what she wanted to be when she was grown up she answered "Everything." Later, she changed "Everything" into firefighter, and now she wants to be an ice cream seller. That last choice makes me feel very lucky to know that I am one of her favorite people.

Out in My Garden

Song with finger puppets

This game is similar to "Who Has the Walnut?", but instead of objects, we use finger puppets which remain visible throughout the game.

Out in my gar-den, un-der a tree, I see a but-ter-fly look-ing at me.

Formation: circle

Preparation:
Place a finger puppet for every child in the middle of the circle. The children name them and choose one.

Activity:
The children sit in a circle with a puppet on their finger. The puppets must be visible to everyone during the course of the game.

The teacher starts the song and chooses a puppet to sing to: "Out in my garden, under a tree, I see a 'black bear' looking at me." The child who has it on her finger chooses another animal to sing to and when she's finished puts her puppet in front of her. The game continues until everyone has had a turn.

The puppets I use are: gorilla, schnauzer, skunk, rabbit, sheep, hedgehog, raccoon, porcupine, cat, black bear, eagle, koala bear, fox, mouse, chipmunk, penguin, hummingbird, dragon, bat and butterfly.

Finger puppets are available on Amazon.com from the company Folkmanis. They are beautiful, as you can see from the picture, and very sturdy.

Rain, Rain, Go Away

Song and Solfège game

The previous three activities use imitation of short melodic motifs as a way of developing pitch perception. The next step is to show the difference in pitch with body gestures.

adapted by
Nicole Hammer

Activity 1

Children sing the song and touch their head on *sol* and their shoulders on *mi* in the first two measures of each line: "Rain, rain, go away…" and "Sun, sun, come and stay…"

Extension

- Find words related to rain and sing them in *sol* and *mi* with the appropriate gestures. Example:

Activity 2

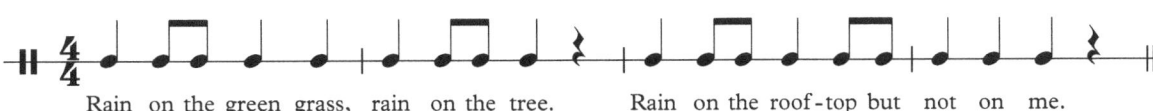

Rain on the green grass, rain on the tree. Rain on the roof-top but not on me.

+ Use the rhyme to play with rain sounds.
  Divide the class in small groups. Each group recites one part of the rhyme and chooses an object, body percussion sound or instrument to imitate the sound of rain as it falls on "grass, tree, rooftop, me." The sound does not have to follow the rhythm of the words.

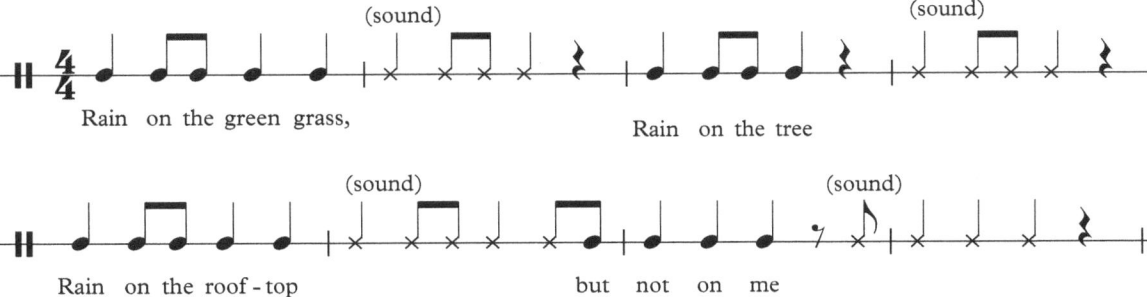

+ Use hula hoops to represent puddles of water.
  One group recites the rhyme; the others jump from hoop to hoop. Anyone who is inside a hoop at the end of the rhyme must sit down to "dry their feet".

Suggested Children's book
Martin, Bill, Archambault, John Endicott James: *Listen to the Rain*. Henry Holt & Co, 1988

This is a book that evokes the different sounds of rain and the quiet when it stops.

Postman

Song and games.
Postman is probably the most favorite game of all the children I have ever worked with. For the teacher it has great advantages as well, since it's an opportunity to hand out pictures of something you want your children to know about or look at while doing it. The game has interesting extensions that make it more physical and creative when the postman delivers pictures of people or stick figures in action and the children are asked to "read" them.

Before you begin
- Prepare as many envelopes as there are children playing the game.
- Choose pictures of subjects that are of interest to the children. Glue each picture on the top half of a sheet of paper, fold the sheet in half and place it in an envelope.
- Choose two "special" pictures to indicate the next postman or the collector of the mail.
- Show the children how to open their envelope, take out the letter, unfold it and "read" it. I usually pretend that I received a real letter and start reading to them: "Dear Madame, It has come to my attention that you are teaching music to a class of children who all have very big noses, seven legs and are extremely silly." This starts five minutes of mayhem of course but I like to tease them in case they think that at school everything has to be serious.
- Make sure to mention that the envelope should not be licked at the end of each session!

Activity
Children and teacher sit in a circle. The postman stands outside the circle with his bag of mail.

When the song starts, the postman places a letter behind each child. The children wait until the last child has received his or her mail before opening their letter.

When the letters are opened and everyone has had time to view their picture and find out if they are the new collector or postman, the "letters" are put back into the envelopes. The new collector picks them up and hands them over to the next postman or postgirl and the game continues.

Extension 1

Guessing an occupation by watching someone perform the action is an old game. I used to play it when I was a child and we called it *Stommen ambacht,* which means "Dumb trade."

+ Use pictures of *people in action* or *people performing a trade* to play a guessing game:

  The game starts the same way with the postman going around.
  Tell the children they are going to imitate what the person is doing in their picture.
  Give them time to look at their picture and mentally prepare for the posture they are going to show.
  The last child to receive her letter stands up and performs her imitation.
  The first child to guess the trade or the action takes the next turn.
  Play until everyone has had a chance to demonstrate their picture.

Examples of people in action

Extension 2

+ Use pictures of stick figures to play a mirror game.

Again the game starts as in the original activity.
Everyone receives a letter with a picture of a stick figure.
When the envelopes are opened, the children look at their picture and memorize it.
One child starts the game by showing the posture of her stick figure, and the other children imitate it.
The game ends when everyone has shown the posture on their card.

Samples of Stick Figures

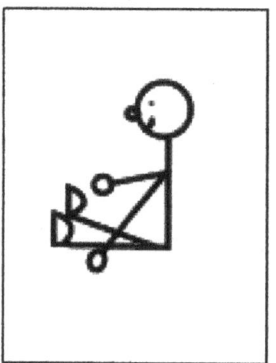 

Jason Wears a Red Shirt

Song

Formation: circle

Activity

Teacher chooses colors that the children are wearing and sings her way around the circle. Children respond with the second sentence and clap to the beat.

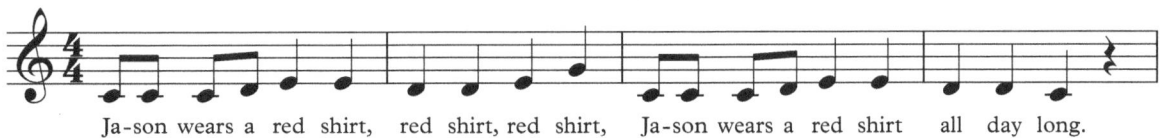

Ja-son wears a red shirt, red shirt, red shirt, Ja-son wears a red shirt all day long.

We will clap for Ja-son, Ja-son, Ja-son, we will clap for Ja-son all day long.

On My Head is a Little Bonnet

Song with finger play

When I was growing up, bonnets and hats were still an important part of everyone's wardrobe. My father never left the house without his hat and my mother, sister and I wore ours on special occasions, like our regular Wednesday afternoon excursions into town. Those weekly visits always ended at "Fritz" which was a posh tea room, a bit like the Russian Tea Room in New York. They served the best waffles in town and for us kids there was the "Coupe Brésilienne," a round, silver plated cup filled to the brim with vanilla ice cream covered with a layer of crunchy roasted hazelnuts and decorated with a crisp, fresh baked wafer. We never once missed going to Fritz because our mom had the biggest sweet tooth in all of Ghent. Arriving there without a hat and gloves was unthinkable.

I learned this song from my grandmother who played it with me long before I could speak. She would take my hand in hers and use the tip of her index finger to touch the tip of my fingers, one by one, while she sang. When she arrived at the last word, "thumb", she would gently squeeze my thumb and smile. I am the oldest of three so I heard all her songs again when she played them with my sister and brother. I played them with my children and grandchildren and now I share them with you.

Play this game on the children's hands as often as you can. It's a very nice way to spend some individual time with them. After a while they will be able to play the game with their friends or do it on their own.

Original Version in Ghent dialect
Adapted and translated by Nicole Hammer

Activity

Hold the child's hand and touch the tip of each finger to the beat of the song. STOP for one beat on each rest.

Thumb = 1 Index finger = 2 Middle finger = 3 Ring finger = 4 Pinky = 5

| On | my | head | is | a | lit - tle | bon - net | and | on | top | a | su - gar | plum |
| 5 | 4 | 3 | 2___ | | 1 2 | 3 4 | 5 | 4 | 3 | 2 | 1 2 | 3 |

Plum plum plum a su - gar plum Here's my fin - ger and there's my thumb.
4   5   4   3 2   1   2   3   4   5___ 4   3   2   1

Extensions

• One, Two, Three, Four Take a Hat!

Sing this song while passing a bag filled with hats around the circle. The child who holds the bag at the end of the song takes a hat and puts it on. The song is an adaptation of a Dutch children's song about a paper hat: "Een twee, drie, vier, hoedje van papier"

Original Flemish version
Adapted and translated by Nicole Hammer

Een, twee, drie, vier, hoed-je van, hoed-je van, een, twee, drie, vier, hoed-je van pa-pier.
One, two, three, four, take a hat, take a hat, one, two, three, four, take a hat.

Heb je dan green hoed-je meer, maak er een-tje van pa-pier. Een twee, drie, vier oed-je van pa-pier.
Choose a bean-ie or a cap, wear a crown or cor-o-net. One, two, three, four, take a hat.

- Make a paper hat out of a sheet of newspaper

SUGGESTED CHILDREN'S BOOKS

Esphyr Slobodkina. *Caps for Sale*. Harper Collins, 1987
Jon Klassen. *This is not My Hat*. Candlewick Press, 2012
Jon Klassen. *I Want My Hat Back*. Candlewick Press, 2011

To Stop the Train

Song with movement

Gestures
Talk about the meaning of "emergency" in the song.
Ask the children to demonstrate different gestures to express the important words of that song.

Example
STOP: hold both hands in front of you palms facing outward
TRAIN: move both arms in a circular motion to imitate the rolling movement of the wheels
CASES OF EMERGENCY: hold both hands up as if trying to get someone's attention
PULL ON THE CHAIN: pull an imaginary handle with one hand
PENALTY FOR IMPROPER USE: point with one finger
FIVE: clap fist into palm of the other hand
POUNDS: open the fist and hold that hand out, ready to receive the fine

Extension
+ Game with chairs and instruments

Preparation
Form a train with an even amount of chairs
Place instruments on the even numbered chairs
The example below uses wood block, drum, rhythm sticks and tambourine

Formation
Children with instruments sit on the even numbered chairs
Children without instruments on odd numbered chairs

Activity
Everyone sings the song. The children without instruments tap the beat (4 per measure) on the shoulders of their friends who transfer the tapping to their instrument.

Note
I found this song in "Very Favorites of the Very Young: Songs for 3-6 year olds", a collection of songs assembled by Carol Henry when she was administrator and teacher at The Creative Preschool, the Montessori school in Spruce Pine, North Carolina.

"To Stop the Train" is listed as a song from James Wild, Barnsley, England.

Suggested songs for Pre-School, Kindergarten and First Grade

A sailor went to sea
Caterpillar crawling by
Cockles and mussels
Coming round the mountain
Gypsy Rover
I'm a little teapot
Itsy bitsy spider
Jamaica farewell
Jennie Jenkins
Kookaburra
Little red caboose
London Bridge
Lucy Locket
Mail myself to you
Miss Mary Mack
My bonnie lies over the ocean
My favorite things.
Old Dan Tucker
Old gray cat
Once I had a pumpkin
Over the river
Paw Paw Patch
Sarasponda.
Shake your sillies out
Skinni Marink

Skip to my Lou
Sur le Pont d' Avignon
Take me out to the ball game
The more we are together
The Muffin Man
The Noble Duke of York
To stop the train
Tommy Thumb
Where's Mary?
Who fed the chickens
Here comes a bluebird
I saw a ghost one night
Shoo fly
We were going to Kentucky
I wrote a letter to my love
Little Johnny Brown
Little Sally Walker
Zodiac
London Bridge is falling down
Down by the station
Johnny works with one hammer
l'Inverno l'è passato
Frère Jacques
In wisdom's lovely splendid ways

Note
- do not sing too loudly
- do not sing too low
- encourage children to sing alone
- choose a repertoire that is varied and fun

Noor's dancing girl (8 years old)

Noor's apple tree (6 years old)

IV. DANCING

When we were growing up, my sister and I danced for our father every night after we were washed and our hair rolled in curlers, and before we ate our bowl of porridge. There was no music to dance to because all we had was a radio and the only dancers we had ever seen were our friends who had ballet lessons, but we twirled and jumped and tip toed just as well. One night, after my sister had announced me as the famous ballerina such and such, I used a "pas de chat" to jump out of the kitchen into the living room and quickly shut the door behind me. I didn't know that my mother was following me with a bowl of porridge in each hand. Well, the good side was that we went to bed that night without having to eat porridge. Our daily dance routine came to a sudden stop when we discovered that our friends had found a hole in our blinds and were peeping in.

IV.1. DANCING TO A SONG

The elements of music and dance are so closely related that dancing is the ideal way to learn the basics of tempo, rhythm, meter, phrasing and form. Other abstract concepts like spiral, curve, circle, contrast, repetition, under, over, beside, through, high, low, etc. are easier to understand when they can be sensed through movement: only through the experience of the action can a child understand the meaning of the corresponding term.

The best way to teach a dance to young children is by just doing it. Talking about it or taking it apart doesn't make sense. Unless there is a tricky move that needs special attention, it is better to sing the song once and go for it. As always, the children will watch you intently because they want to do every move exactly as the teacher does. Slowly but surely they will also sing the song.

I don't think I have ever given a music class without some dancing in it because I know the children love it and I do too.

TRADITIONAL AMERICAN SONGS

A long time ago, a lot of people lived on farms and it was hard for boys and girls to meet as the farms were far apart. Therefore, their parents organized big parties where they could sing and dance together. The music was often played on violins or flutes by travelling musicians but if there was nobody who could play an instrument, the boys and girls would dance to their own singing. They made sure they learned a lot of songs, because the more they knew, the more dancing they could do.

Shoo Fly

Shoo fly don't both-er me Shoo fly don't both-er me Shoo fly don't both-er me 'cause I be-long to some-bod-y. I feel, I feel, I feel like the morn-ing star. I feel, I feel, I feel like the morn-ing star.

Formation
Circle holding hands

Activity

Shoo fly, don't bother me, shoo fly, don't bother me
(Take three steps to the center, feet together on "me", three steps back, feet together on "me")

Shoo fly, don't bother me for I belong to somebody
(same as above)

I feel, I feel, I feel like the morning star.
(Somebody breaks the circle and takes the line of children under the arch formed by the raised arms of the child next to him and his neighbor. The line follows the leader and keeps moving, making a big loop, until everyone is back in their spot)

Jump Jim Joe

Formation
Two children stand in the middle of the circle, holding hands.

Activity

Jump, jump, jump Jim Joe
(jump on each word)

shake your head
(shake head)

and nod your head
(nod)

and tap your toe
(tap three times)

Round, around, around we go
(two-hand turn with partner)

'till we find another partner
(take a new partner)

and we jump Jim Joe
(jump three times with your new partner if you have time)

Play the game until all the children are dancing and have the opportunity to switch partners a few times.

Note
Some dances are simple enough for all children to start at once and this is one of them. I prefer a slower beginning where one couple starts and invites someone new, each time doubling the amount of dancers. This works very well with younger children and they like it that way.

SONGS FROM OTHER COUNTRIES

L'inverno l'è Passato

Song from Ticino, Switzerland

L'in-ver-no l'è pas-sa-to l'a-pri-le non c'è più è mag-gio è ri-tor-na-to al can-to del cu-cù. Cu-cù cu-cù l'a-pri-le non c'è più è ri-tor-na-to è mag-gio al can-to del cu-cù.

Formation
Circle holding hands

Preparation
This is a song about the joy of knowing that winter is over (L'Inverno l'è passato), that April is past,(l'aprile non c'è più) that the month of May has returned, (e maggio è ritornato) and with it, the song of the cuckoo, (al canto del cucù.)

Activity

L'Inverno l'è passato, l'aprile non c'è più
(walk CW to the beat of the song)

e maggio è ritornato al canto del cucù.
(walk CCW, face the center at "cucù")

Cucù, cucù,
(take four steps the center)

l'aprile non c'è più
(take four steps back)

e ritornato è maggio, al canto del cucù
(drop hands, circle in place with small steps and face the center on "cucù")

Frère Jacques

Song from France

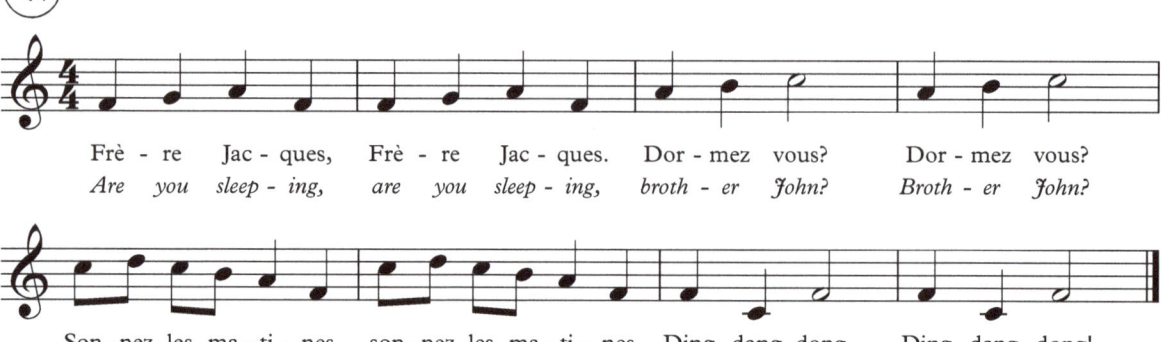

Frè - re Jac - ques, Frè - re Jac - ques. Dor - mez vous? Dor - mez vous?
Are you sleep - ing, are you sleep - ing, broth - er John? Broth - er John?

Son - nez les ma - ti - nes, son - nez les ma - ti - nes. Ding, dang, dong Ding, dang, dong!
Morn-ing bells are ring-ing, morn-ing bells are ring-ing. Ding, dang, dong Ding, dang, dong!

Formation
circle, holding hands

Activity

Frère Jacques, frère Jacques,
(walk CW)

Dormez-vous? Dormez vous?
(walk CCW)

Sonnez les matines! Sonnez les matines!
(take four steps to the middle and four steps back)

Ding, dang, dong. Ding dang, dong.
(swing arms to each bell sound)

Note

Sing the song in the original language. Young children are very good at speaking other languages even if they don't understand the meaning of the words.

San Isidro Labrador

Song from Spain

I learned this beautiful song and the corresponding activities from watching a workshop by Sofia Lopez-Ibor called "El Pelele - Spanish Games." I very much like the way Sofia teaches the activity by starting with the movement rather than the singing. The children are first physically involved in the process through body percussion and movement and even though they are not asked to sing, they do so very quickly because they always imitate the teacher. They learn words and music in no time, without pressure.

San Isidro is the patron saint of Madrid who brings the best harvest and many other good things to the people as we see from the next three verses. The song and especially the third line where a pig is slaughtered reminded me of the time that I lived with my family in the Flemish countryside. Every year after the harvest was collected and stored, the farmer, who was also my landlord, would ask the butcher to slaughter one of his pigs. The meat was immediately cut and stored and the next day he invited family and friends to dinner. The meal was prepared with the parts of the pig they could not store and served with potatoes, berries, apples and veggies from the garden and a lot of that excellent beer Flanders is famous for. For anybody who still had some space left, there were coffee, freshly baked waffles or rice pudding for desert. I remember walking home afterwards along the fields with my husband and children, promising myself I wouldn't eat for at least a week.

Spanish Song

Preparation

The structure or form of this song is AB[1]. Use it to create a dance with two contrasting parts.

    A. Walk by yourself
    B. Choose a partner and circle around while holding hands.

---

1 To understand the structure of a song or dance, we use capital letters (A,B,C, etc.) to designate the different sections.

Formation
Children stand in circle, one child on the inside.

Activity
A

San Isidro labrador la cosecha es la mejor (2x)
(Child on the inside walks around, and stops in front of a child at the end of the phrase)

B

Pun cata pun cata pun chin pun, gori, gori, gori surum sum sum (2x)
(Both children hold hands and circle in one direction on the first phrase and change direction on the repeat)

Children separate. They walk by themselves on A and choose a new partner from the circle on B. The game is repeated until everyone is participating.

Extension 1
A. Walk by yourself
B. Children find new ways to make contact with their partner. Instead of holding hands, they can hook arms, touch elbows, put their hands on each other's shoulders, etc.

Extension 2
A. Walk by yourself
B. Face your partner, and use body percussion and movements to accompany the syllables. The examples are from Sofia's workshop.

Pun (Clap)
ka-ta (Pat L and R)
chin (Clap partner's hands)
gori gori gori (Circle hands one around the other)
surum sum sum (palms of hands together, hands open like a flower, arms slowly moving upwards)

Gori gori   Surum-sum-sum

Use an echo game with Pun, ka-ta, and chin to teach the rhythmic elements of the B part

Echo games are very popular in Orff Schulwerk. They are used to challenge children to imitate rhythms and involve accurate listening and memory. The teacher demonstrates one sentence at a time and the children imitate. The ones that are not properly reproduced are repeated.

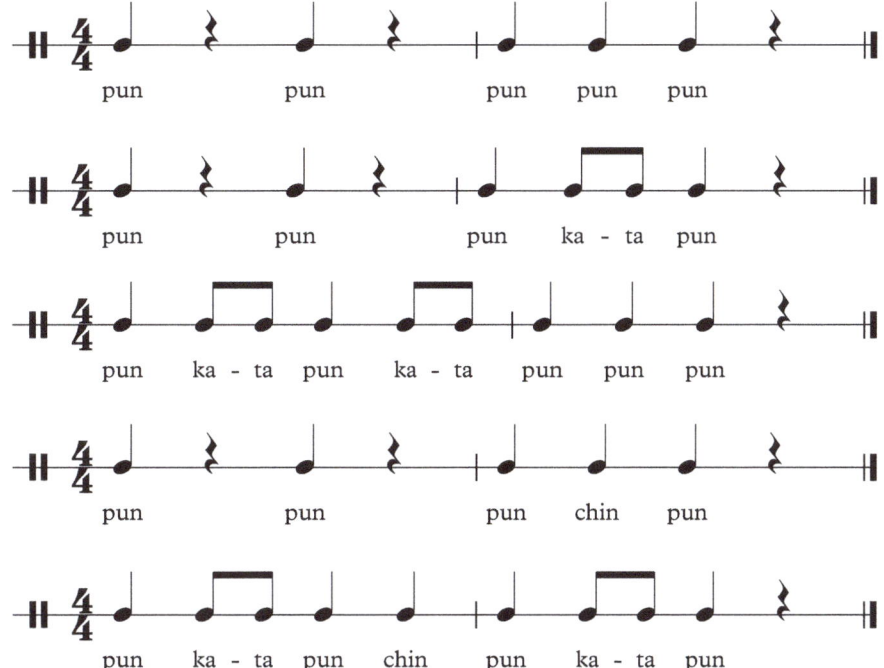

Perform the complete song with body percussion, movement and singing.

Walk by yourself on the A part, stop before a partner and do the body percussion and gestures on B. Repeat the same verse until everyone is dancing.

Note
Depending on the level of your students, use the other verses of the song.

A la ermita de San Antonio todos van a buscar novio
In the church of San Antonio, all pray for a boyfriend

En la case del vecino han matado un buen cochino
In the neighbor's house a pig has been killed

Subiremos a las zancos para poder ser mas altos
We will stand on stilts to be bigger

Sharpen Your Knives and Scissors

Song from Flanders

When I was growing up in Ghent, it was safe to play in our street. The only traffic coming through was the occasional horse-drawn cart on its way to the smithy or push carts from the different peddlers. Every Friday, the fishmonger came, pushing his cart with one hand and spinning a rattle with the other. He sold sole, plaice and mussels lying on a bed of seaweed. The knife and scissor sharpener showed up once a month, to the excitement of all the kids in the neighborhood. Like the baker and the milk man, he had a dog cart on which he had installed his equipment, and to do the job, he pushed a pedal that turned the wheel of his wet stone. As soon as the knife touched the stone, the sparks went flying and we jumped and ran to avoid getting stung by them. His dog was underneath the cart, well away from danger, taking advantage of the break to have a snooze.

Baker's cart

Milk cart

Sharpen Your Knives and Scissors

Translated and adapted by
Nicole Hammer

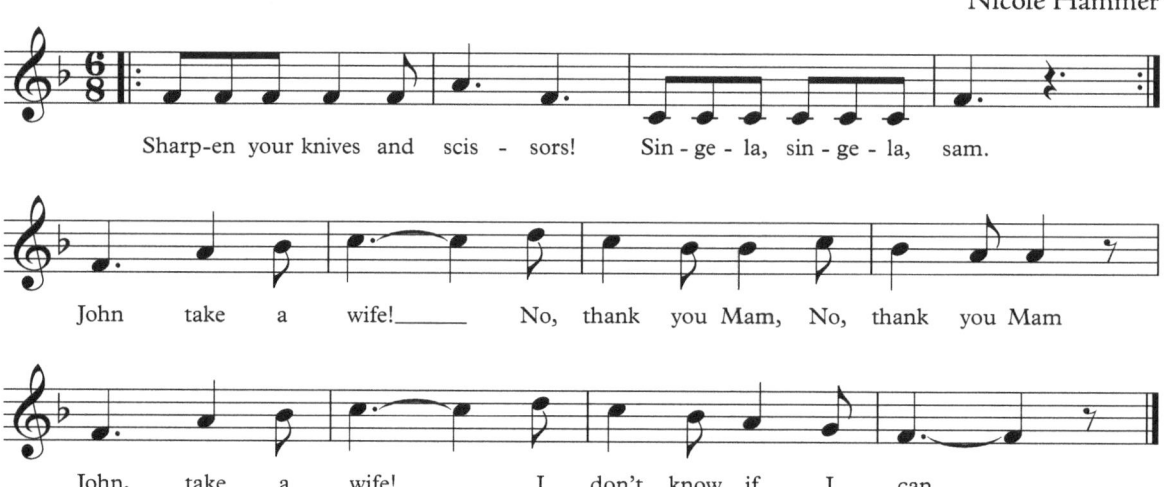

Formation
Form a circle of partners holding hands, facing CW.

Activity
The structure of the song is AB.
　　A. Walk and stop to face partner at the end of the repeat.
　　B. Children on the outside of the circle play the "Mam" part; children on the inside play "John."
　　At the end, every "John" moves one spot up the line to the next "Mam" on "I don't know if I can."

Sharpen your knives and scissors, Singela, singela, sam! (2x)
(Partners walk CW in circle and face each other on the second "sam")

John take a wife!
(Outside children shake their index finger at their partner on each beat)

No thank you Mam, No thank you Mam.
(Inside children cross their arms in front of their chest and shake their head)

John take a wife!
(Same as previous)

I don't know if I can
(Inside children move one spot up the line and join hands with their new partner)

The game continues until all the children have danced with each other

Extension

+ Create a speech ostinato to accompany the song. Divide the class in two groups, one sings the song the others speak the ostinato.

+ Rub two wooden blocks covered on one side with sandpaper against each other. Do it in one short movement on each rest in the ostinato.

SONGS BASED ON STORIES

Children like to play pretend games that reflect what happens in their lives, the stories they hear, the books they read and the programs they watch. During my childhood we played "Mother and Father," "Cowboys and Indians" and "Tea Party" but our favorite game was "Statues in the Shop". There was a shop owner, his client and some very peculiar statues. These were created by the shop owner taking hold of their hand, spinning them around and letting go. After the statue recovered its balance it assumed a pose, but nobody knew what it represented. The fun started when the client came in. After saying "triiiiing," he was welcomed by the owner who showed him all his statues, always informing him that he didn't know what they were because "they had just come in that day!" The client picked one, and the shop owner pressed a button on its head. This made the statue come alive and turn into a dancing ballerina or most often a dangerous wolf, ghost or robot gone mad. Depending on his luck, the client would either wait for his statue to be wrapped up or flee the store, pursued by this wild creature. Only the shopkeeper could stop it by pressing the button on its head, which it tried to avoid at all cost.

Noor's dancing girl and boy (8 years old)

Thorn Rosa

Thorn Ro-sa was a pret-ty child, a pret-ty child, a pret-ty child Thorn Ro-sa was a pret-ty child a pret-ty child.

Preparation
Read the text of the song to see if the children recognize the story of "Sleeping Beauty."

Formation
Circle, holding hands. The wicked witch and the prince are outside the circle. Thorn Rosa stands in the center.

Costumes and props
Cape, hat and sword for the prince. Cape and hat for the wicked witch. Mantle, crown and necklace for the princess.

Activity
Thorn Rosa was a pretty child, a pretty child, a pretty child…
(The children join hands and circle around Thorn Rosa)

She grew up in a castle high…
(They stand still and raise their arms)

One day there came a wicked witch…
(The wicked witch walks around the circle)

The wicked witch said: Fall asleep…
(The witch sneaks inside the circle and points her finger at Thorn Rosa)

Thorn Rosa slept for a hundred years…
(Thorn Rosa falls asleep, the children circle around)

The thorny bush grew giant high…
(The children imitate a bush slowly growing and keep their arms raised at the end)

One day there came a handsome prince…

(The prince walks around the circle, the children keep their arms raised)

He cut right through the thorny bush...
(The prince gently touches each child's back with his sword, to "cut them down." Once the "bush" is on the floor, the prince enters the circle)

He woke Thorn Rosa with a kiss...
(The prince kisses or touches Thorn Rosa who wakes up. All children stand up and join hands)

My queen will be Thorn Rosa...
(The prince bows to Thorn Rosa, while the children circle around)

Extension

Choose a partner and walk to the *Gavotte des Festins* from *Marches, Fêtes & Chasses pour Louis XIV* from André Philidor played by the Symphonie du Marais" conducted by Hugo Reyne. Track 22. Available on Amazon.com

When the play is finished, everyone pairs up behind Thorn Rosa and her Prince and walks in procession to the beat of this stately dance.

Gavotte is the name of a dance that was popular during the time of Louis XIV.

In this rendition, the part for trumpet sounds a little shaky and off key sometimes, because it is a "natural" trumpet. The natural trumpet is different from the modern one and much harder to play. Only very skilled musicians can tackle it.

Note

During all the years that I have played this game I have been amazed by the commitment of the children to play their roles with the gravity of professional actors. The princesses lay motionless on the floor from the moment they fall until the prince kisses or touches them. The princes are always dignified and never abuse their position to poke someone with their sword. The role of witch or wizard is as popular as the other two, and although the part is small, every witch or wizard has patiently waited outside the circle for the end of the story.

Louise was 6 years old when she drew this picture and when asked who these queens were said "That's me and Mama." Someone pointed to the smallest one and said, "So this is you!" and she answered: "NO! This is Mama!"

Making Capes for Thorn Rosa, the Prince and the Wicked Witch or Wizard.

When I was a child, my grandmother taught me how to sew which enabled me to make simple garments for the dress-up box in the music class. The following two capes can be used for princes and princesses, soldiers, hunters, witches or wizards, fairies, etc. depending on the fabric or the color. Choose fabric that does not wrinkle, and you will have a trunk full of clothes that always look good. Add crowns and necklaces, hats, swords and wands, and make a lot of children very happy.

Pattern for Thorn Rosa cape

1. Cut a piece of soft tulle into the right length and width.

2. Fold in half lengthwise.

3. Gather to a width of 18' at the height shown on the drawing. Pin the gathering to keep it in place.

4. Prepare a piece of ribbon. Sew it on top of the gathering.

5. Attach two big safety pins on each side of the ribbon. They allow the teacher to pin the cape to the back of "Thorn Rosa's" dress or T-shirt. They stay attached to the garment when it is taken off.

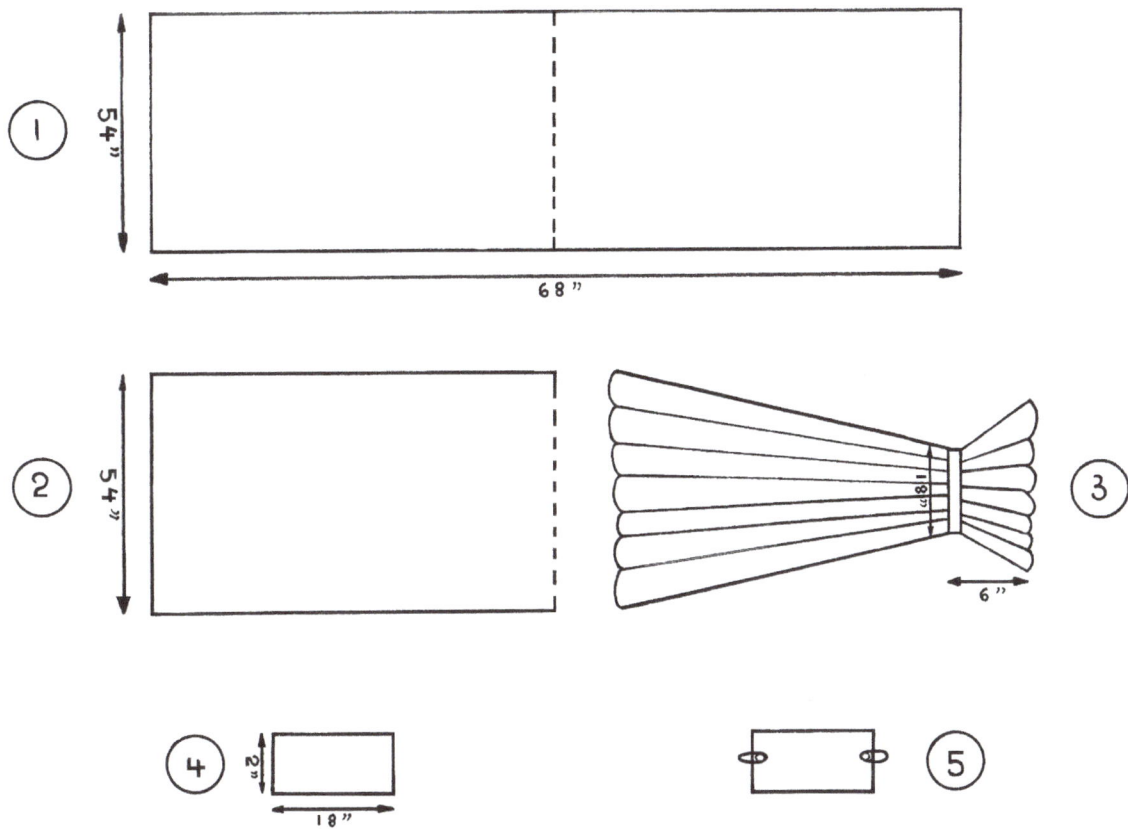

Pattern of cape for the wicked witch, wizard or prince

Choose fabric that does not need to be hemmed, like fleece for example or certain kinds of velvet.

1. Cut a circle of 45' wide and 48' long.

Look for the center of the fabric (indicated by a dot on the picture) and use a 45' long string of cotton thread to trace a circle with a piece of chalk. Hold one end of the string in the dot and use the other end to trace the circle.

2. Trace a smaller circle in the middle of your circle with a diameter of 5' for the neckline.

Before you cut it out, cut a straight opening from the circumference of the largest circle to the circumference of the smaller circle you just traced. Once you have cut an opening in the cape it is easier to cut out the neckline. Voila, you already have a cape.

3. and 4. Cut one piece of 2' by 19' and two pieces of 1' by 20' from the left over fabric. Sew the widest piece around the neckline.

Place it against and even with the edge of the neckline and sew it on. Turn it to the inside and attach it with a slip stitch. Keep both ends open; slip one of the longer strips of fabric in each one. Attach with a couple of stitches.

5. If your fabric does not fray, you're done.

IV. Dancing

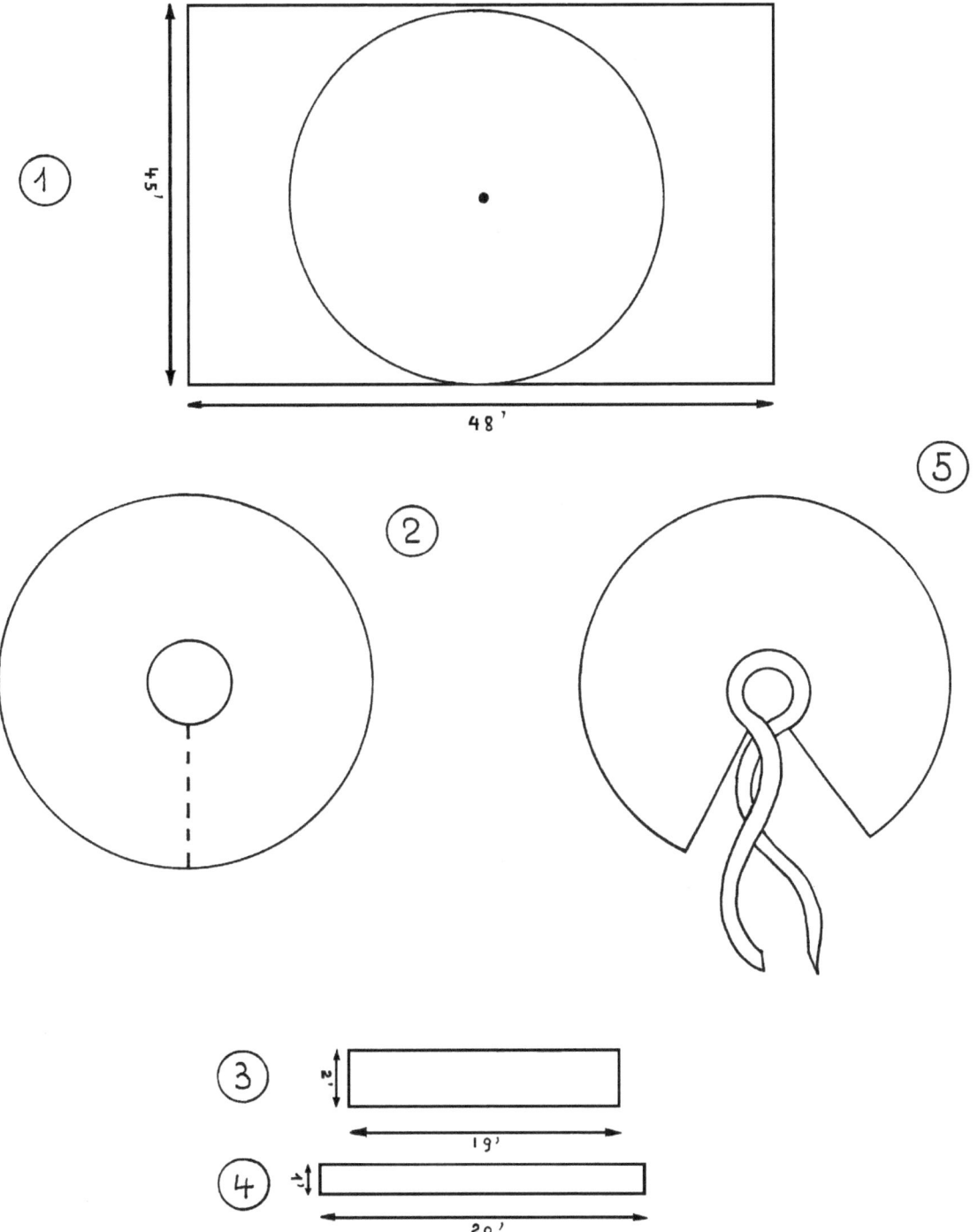

Capes for the witch or wizard and the Prince.

SONGS FROM THE AFRO-AMERICAN HERITAGE
Little Johnny Brown

I learned the following movement activity at a Jazz workshop given by Doug Goodkin, whose books and workshops are a treasure trove of musical ideas and an excellent model of Orff-Schulwerk.

The song also appears in Bessie Jones' *Step it Down: Games, Plays, Songs and Stories*[1] from the Afro-American Heritage. She was a gospel singer honored by the National Endowment for the Arts. "Step it Down" is a testament to her love of music and her heritage.

In this simplified version of the movement game, children pretend to be an animal, and they always take this role more seriously than any other bit of acting. It seems as if they are no longer aware they are pretending and they hypnotize their friends with the intensity on their faces and solemn dignity in their movements even if it's impossible to recognize what animal they are portraying.

Preparation
Demonstrate how to place a scarf flat on the floor. Turn each corner towards the center and say: "First corner, second corner, third corner, fourth corner" as you walk around the scarf. Stoop down each time you fold a corner.

Formation
Circle. One child in the middle holding a scarf by two upper corners.

Activity
Children sing while child in the middle performs the actions.

Little Johnny Brown, lay your comfort down (2x)
(hold the scarf by two corners and slowly place it flat on the floor)

Turn the first (second, third, fourth) corner, Johnny Brown
(walk around the scarf and stoop down each time to turn a corner)

Tell everyone which animal you want to imitate.
Continue

Walk like a "chicken" Johnny Brown
(walk around the scarf and show your motion)

Give it to your best friend, Johnny Brown
(pick up scarf and give it to somebody in the circle)

Other choices that often come up are: *fly like an eagle, hop like a bunny or a frog, crawl like a snake, walk like a tiger, elephant, giraffe and cat, slither like a snake.*

---

1 Jones, Bessie and Lomax Hawkes, Bess. *Step it Down*. Athens, Georgia. The University of Georgia Press, 1972.

IV. Dancing

African-American Song

Lit-tle John-ny Brown lay your com-fort down.

Lit-tle John-ny Brown lay your com-fort down.

Turn the first cor-ner John-ny Brown_ Turn the sec-ond cor-ner John-ny Brown_

Turn the third cor-ner John-ny Brown_ Turn the fourth cor-ner John-ny Brown_

Walk like a li-on John-ny Brown_ Walk like a li-on John-ny Brown_

Give it to your best friend John-ny Brown_ Give it to your best friend John-ny Brown_

Note

This activity is perfect for children who are too shy to stand in the circle by themselves. The ritual of placing a scarf on the floor and turning down all the corners one by one gives them the courage to start.

IV.2. DANCING TO RECORDED MUSIC

Dancing to recorded music is more challenging than dancing to one's own rhyme or song. The musical structure which feels so clearly divided into phrases when one sings or speaks them seems less defined. But children are born to dance and they usually have no problem switching from one to the other.

CLASSICAL MUSIC

The Princess and the Goblin
A dance for two hand puppets
Music: *Hungarian Dance No. 3* by J. Brahms

Preparation
The form and character of this music lend themselves perfectly to a simple game between two characters, a princess puppet and a goblin puppet (see art project below).

The first melody (A) is sweet and light, representing the Princess. The second (B) is darker and heavier, played by the goblin.

After they each appear twice, a different, threatening melody (C) comes in and then slowly disappears. The music ends with the first theme.

The form of this piece is AA BB AA BB CB AA

Formation
Circle. The children hold the princess puppet in one hand and the goblin puppet in the other behind their back. They need to remember which hand holds the princess and which holds the goblin.

Activity
AA   the princess appears and dances so that she is always visible to everyone else
BB   the goblin appears to dance and the princess quickly disappears
AA   the princess comes back and the goblin disappears
BB   goblin returns; princess exits
  C   the music speeds up, the princess comes out and uses the strong rhythm in this section to say, "Goblin, please go away!" She says it four times
  B   the goblin slowly goes away as the music fades
AA   the princess happily resumes her dancing and bows at the end

Art Project

Draw a princess and a goblin and color them. Cut out, glue onto lollypop sticks and use them as your puppets.

Noor's goblin and princess (7 years old)

SUGGESTED CHILDREN'S BOOKS

Melissa Sweet. *Balloons over Broadway: The True Story of the Puppeteer of Macy's Parade*. HMH Books for Young Readers, 2011

Ed Young and Hillary Beckett. *The Rooster's Horns: A Chinese Puppet Play to Make and Perform*. (UNICEF Storycraft Book). HMH Books for Young Readers, 2011

Papillons (Butterflies)

Papillons and *March of the Lions* are the only free dances in the book because children are already very good at it. But sometimes a piece of music is irresistible, like this jewel for piano by Robert Schumann. That, along with the children's fondness for a certain finger puppet and the challenge to dance in such a way that the butterfly moves its wings up and down provide an opportunity not to be missed.

Papillons: Op. 2 no. 7 (*Semplice*) by Robert Schumann (Christian Zacharias, piano)

Activity 1
- Children put a butterfly finger puppet on a middle finger.
- Move to the music while flapping the butterfly's wings.[1]

Extension
- Use two scarves, one in each hand instead of the butterfly puppet.

Activity 2
Use scarves to play a movement game without music.

Divide the class in 2 groups: one group thinks about different ways to make a butterfly move, the other group executes the movements with a scarf in each hand.

Examples:
- Changing from caterpillar into butterfly
- Butterfly caught in a net
- Butterfly caught in a rainstorm
- Butterfly drinking nectar from a flower

---

[1] The butterfly finger puppet is available on Amazon.com from Folkmanis. It is beautiful, easy to put on and very sturdy.

IV. Dancing

Suggested Children's Books
Horacek Pete, *Butterfly, Butterfly: A book of colors* Cambridge, Massachusetts: 2007
Carley, Eric, *The Very Hungry Caterpillar* New York: Philomel Books, 1969

DANCE MUSIC COMPOSED FOR CHILDREN

Highway No. 1

The exciting music of the Australian group the "Shenanigans" is a great addition to the dance repertoire of the Preschool, Kindergarten and First Grade classroom. Highway no. 1 is a song about driving by car through Australia and stopping at several cities. At each stop, a child's voice invites us to show a different movement.

Highway No. 1: from the collection *Children's Dances of Terra Del Zur*. Shenanigans

Activity

- Children are spread across the room, ready to take off as soon as they hear the engine start.
- Steer the car around the room, push the brakes at the word "stop" and follow the instructions:
    Walk, walk and run, run, run.
    Heel and toe and stamp.
    Side, together, wiggle.
    Jump, jump and clap, clap, clap.
    Skip, skip and bow.
    Gallop, gallop, jump.
    Hop, hop, hop and stop.

Les Saluts

The music of the New England Dancing Masters and their intensive experience in the classroom makes their music indispensable in Preschool, Kindergarten and Primary Grades

Les Saluts: from the collection "Listen to the Mockingbird" by the New England Dancing Masters Production (Amidon, Brass and Davis).

Les Saluts is French for *The Bows* or *The Greetings* and indicates that the dancers bow to three things "worthy of respect." The notion of "respect" is not well known to young children and it is easier to ask them what they like the most in the classroom OR what the things or people are they would miss the most if they were not there.

Activity 1

The structure of the dance is as follows:
    AA   skip freely around the room
     B   bow to three of your favorite things and clap three times at the end.
The basic form AAB is repeated six times.

Activity 2

Decide on a number of "statues" like ballerina, soldier, statue of liberty, etc. The children show each posture until everyone can easily demonstrate the difference.
    AA   skip freely around the room
     B   the teacher calls "Soldier," "Ballerina," "Statue of liberty" on each one of the three bows and the children assume the pose. They end with three claps.

MUSIC FROM AROUND THE WORLD

Folk instruments are easy to listen to and the character of the music— its simplicity and style—is appealing to children. Use the following activities as an introduction to the world of instruments and a variety of cultures.

Folk dancing is one of the most effective ways to awaken a child's mind to beat, meter, rhythm, melody, phrasing and form and other things such as language and kinesthetic intelligence.

The following dances have one important element in common: they are based on a form that consists of two contrasting tempos. Each dance highlights this contrast in a different way.

Kukuvicka
Bulgarian Dance

Music from *Bush Dances of New Holland* by the Shenanigans.

Formation
Line

Activity
The dance starts with a short introduction, followed by a slow part A and a fast part B.
The dance form is: Intro, A B, A B, A B

Movement
Intro: Wait for the dance to start
Part A: hold a scarf in one hand and slowly walk to the music behind the leader
Part B: skip and raise one arm to wave the scarf

Extension
Place 3 different colored scarves in the center of the circle and invite the children to choose one
Start the dance and use the intro to call a color. The children who have that color follow the teacher
When the second part starts, call the next color to join the group. Repeat for the third and last part

Note
Scarves can be found at West Music in sets of 12. They are seamed, colorful and sturdy.

La Torototelle

Music from *Dance Music for Children* by the Shenanigans. Level 1.
One of the instruments in the ensemble is the accordion

Formation

Partners, in no particular order, holding hands

Activity

This dance has two parts: A is slow and B is fast
A: *Step-close* (to the right), *step-close* (to the left)
This is a pre-waltz step, where the partners hardly move away from their original position
B: Partners let go of their hands and skip freely around the room
At the end of part B, the children must be back in their original place, find their partner and start part A again

Extension

Listen to the ACCORDION (France)
Plaisirs d'amour: French song from *Les Compagnons d'Accordeon*: 20 French Melodies from The World of France, track no. 4, available on Amazon.

"Plaisirs" is a slow waltz, like part A of La Torototelle.

Carnavalito

Music from *Bush Dances of New Holland* by the Shenanigans.
   One of the instruments in the ensemble is the Charango.

The dance starts with a short introduction, followed by a slow part A and a fast part B.
The dance form is: Intro, A B A B A B

Activity
Divide the children into two groups.
Group A is seated and plays rhythm sticks. The rhythm is "One, two, tie my shoe"
Group B dances while playing bells and shakers. Switch

Extension
Listen to the charango, a small string instrument of Bolivia made from an armadillo shell.
   The selected piece is *Cumbre* (Summit) from Sukay Records: *High Energy Music of the Andes*, track no. 2

ACTIVITIES BASED ON A STORY

The next activities are inspired by *The Lion Who Saw Himself in the Water*, a story written by Idries Shah who spent many years collecting tales from all over the world.

Part of our job as preschool and kindergarten teachers is to nurture the natural expressiveness of our young students by practicing a wide variety of facial expressions and gestures. As tools for the development of communication skills, they are now more important than ever, given how much time children spend connected to electronic media. The following games can be used for just such a purpose.

The Lion Who Saw Himself in the Water
Story by Idries Shah. Hoopoe book series of ISHK

This story is about a lion that sees his reflection in a pool and is frightened by the wild creature staring back at him. He is so scared that he does not dare to drink.

Activity

- Read the story and start a discussion by sharing thoughts and ideas. Use the situation where the jungle animals are scared because they think that Share the Lion is too angry and talk about emotions. Ask the children what scares them or makes them angry and invite them to show these and other emotions using facial expressions and body postures.
- Use the image of Share the Lion looking at his reflection in a pool to play a "reflection" or "mirror game" with the emotions the children have shared.

    One child performs an emotion (happy, sad, worried, angry, excited, surprised, or bored) and the other children imitate it and guess which one it is.

    One child shows an emotion and another shows the opposite (happy-sad, angry-friendly)

Extensions

- Create a Play Center with finger puppets to recreate the story. An excellent source for puppets is the company Folkmanis. They have an African wildlife set with many of the animals that appear in the book.

    African Wildlife Play set: elephant, lion, giraffe and zebra.
    Monarch Butterfly. You can find both on Amazon.

IV. Dancing

Good Morning Mister Lion

This is a delightful game that focuses on listening. A "lion" that is blindfolded finds his friend by listening to the sound of an instrument he is playing. It is an interesting experience not only for the children but the teacher as well because it reveals different levels of auditory faculties: some children go directly to the source of the sound while others start to move in the opposite direction and need more time to orient themselves. In my years as a teacher, I haven't found that any of the children who were confused about the location of the sound had hearing problems.

Nicole Hammer

Activity

- Children sit in a circle. One child, the "lion," is blindfolded and stands inside the circle. Once the lion is blindfolded, another child quietly takes up a position outside the circle, ready to play an instrument.

Everyone sings the song and when they are finished, the child on the outside plays his instrument and the "lion" starts searching. The children in the circle get out of his way to let him pass. As soon as the lion touches his friend he takes off his blindfold and they both choose someone to take their place.

Extensions
- Listen to tracks from *Heart of the Forest*: The Music of the Baka Forest People of Southeast Cameroon.

This listening activity ties in with the foregoing one because for the Baka, who live in the heart of the African rainforest, the skill of listening is crucial for their survival. From early on they acquire a great sense of hearing so they can find their way by "listening to the forest." They learn to recognize not only the sounds made by the animals that surround them, but also those from different streams, rivers and even trees. They are a most remarkable people and their music opens a window into an intriguing world.

Track 1-3: Yelli
A group of women get together before dawn and while the men and children are still in their huts, they sing. One voice starts a beautiful melody that reverberates through the trees. Soon another voice joins in and then another. Each voice sings its own repeating melody and the combination of voices carries far into the forest to blend with the nighttime sound of the insects.

Track 4 or 5: Water Drums
It is morning and a group of women take their daily bath in the river. We hear them slap and beat their hands in the water to create an extraordinary variety of rhythmic and melodic sounds.

- Play a listening game involving all children at once.

  Ask the children to spread out in the room and pretend to be a tree or an animal in the jungle. They use a small percussion instrument or their voice to make a sound when a blindfolded child has to pass them to walk from one side of the room to the other. The sound will prevent her from bumping into anyone.

- Share as much information with your children as you can about these remarkable people. This topic could be shared with your colleagues and turned into a project covering many different subjects.

Note
When you listen to this recording it will be hard to choose which track to bring to class because each one is a gem in itself. Tracks 1–6 have always been an integral part of my music class. I usually start the activity by showing a picture of an elephant almost completely hidden by the luxurious undergrowth of the forest. This picture, more than anything brings home the importance of listening. You can find the CD on Amazon.com.

Introduction and Royal March of the Lions

Music
Introduction and *Royal March of the Lions* (1st movement from *Carnival of the Animals* by Camille Saint Saens) written for 2 pianos and orchestra.

Preparation
Class listens to the music.

Form:

Intro:	Tremolo on the piano, string section enters. The music gets louder and louder to a climax with a descending scale on the piano
Stately march of the lions:	Intro by piano, followed by the strings. The same phrase is played four times
Lions roar:	Four up and down scales on the piano, strings join the last two
Lions walk softly and jump:	Piano, strings interrupt; jumps suggested by the strings
Last roar:	On the piano

Questions
Which instrument do you hear first? (piano)

Raise your hand when The March of the Lions begins

Raise your hand when you hear the lions roar (up and down scales on the piano)

Which instrument is playing when the lions roar? (piano)

Which instrument do you hear last, piano or violins? (piano)

Dance

Formation
All the dancers wear a lion mask and are hidden from view

Activity
The music begins with a slow introduction. This short section allows the lions to come on stage.

When the stately march starts, the lions move/dance freely.

Noor the lion

Note

During any kind of dancing, especially free dancing, young children look at the teacher for clues. Be prepared and have fun!

Here's a lion mask that I found on Amazon.com. It looks good and does not cover the mouth.

Suggested Children's Books

De Vos Philip and Grobler Piet, *Carnival of the Animals*, Lemniscaat Imprint of Boyds Mills Press 1996

EPILOGUE

Mom in front of our house.

As I was writing this book it struck me how much my childhood had a bearing on my relationship with my young students and the content and organization of my music classes. Costumes and props, puppets, jazz, classical and folk music, illustrations of art work and the joy of improvising have always been an important part of it. (I almost forgot the pancakes, waffles and muffins!)

Growing up amidst the destruction of WWII, I learned the value of creativity. Many houses on our street, including ours were destroyed. For a while we lived close by and as soon as the war ended Dad started rebuilding on the same spot. We were the first ones to move back and for several years our house was surrounded by rubble. We had lost everything and as a consequence we had no toys to play with but I remember thinking how lucky we were to have so much stuff around us we could just pick up and use to make things.

One of the most important gifts my parents gave us was the freedom to play outside with our friends from the neighborhood with very little supervision. Grandma, who was always knitting or sewing, kept watch from the window overlooking the street but she never interfered, no matter how hard we screamed or quarreled. Scraped knees and elbows were quickly washed with soap and water and a bloody nose was treated with a cold soup spoon in the back of your neck. When it was time for lunch, Mom brought plates of food outside and she was famous for her pancakes or thin slices of bread, smeared with lots of butter and brown sugar.

My father's love of art and music, Grandma's sewing skills, Mom's yummy treats and my joyful memories are all part of this book. I hope you enjoy them as much as I enjoyed writing about them.

Me, Hugo, my sister Pati, Jeannine and Josiane.

BIBLIOGRAPHY AND DISCOGRAPHY

Music and Dance
Keller Wilhelm. *Introduction to Orff Schulwerk:* Schott 1974

Music for Children: Orff-Schulwerk - American Edition, Vol. 1 and 2. Coordinated by Hermann Regner. Schott 1982

Henry Carol. *Very Favorites of the Very Young: Songs for 3-6 Year Olds:* World around Songs. 1986

Haselbach Barbara. *Dance education: Basic Principles and Models for Nursery and Primary School.* Schott 1971

Gunild Keetman. *First Acquaintance with Orff Schulwerk.* Schott 1970

Harding James. *From Wibbleton to Wobbleton.* Pentatonic Press 2013

Goodkin, Doug. *Play, Sing, and Dance: An introduction to Orff Schulwerk.* Schott-EAMC, 2002

Goodkin Doug. *A Rhyme in Time. Rhythm, Speech activities and Improvisation for the Classroom.* Warner Bros. Publications 1997

Lopez Sofia. *Blue is the Sea.* Pentatonic Press 2011

Children's Rhymes, Poetry and Games
Opie, Iona and Peter. *The Oxford Dictionary of Nursery Rhymes.* England. Oxford University Press. 1997

Opie, Iona and Peter. *The Lore and Language of Schoolchildren.* U.S.A. The New York Review of Books. 2001

Opie, Iona and Peter. *Children's Games in Street and Playground* Vol.1 and 2. England. Floris Books. 2008

Opie Iona and Peter. *The Oxford Nursery Rhyme Book.* England. Oxford University Press. 1955.

Children's Books
Shah, Idries. *The Lion who saw Himself in the Water.* U.S.A. Hoopoe Books. 2002

Dance CD'S

Children's Dances of Terra Del Zur. The Best of the Shenanigans. Vol. 1. Australia: Shenanigans
Bush Dances of New Holland. The Best of the Shenanigans. Vol. 2. Australia: Shenanigans
Dance Music for Children Level 1. Australia. Shenanigans
Listen to the Mockingbird: More Dances for Children, School and Communities. U.S.A. New England Dancing Masters Production.

Folk Music CD'S

Cumbre. High Energy Music of the Andes. Sukay Records
The World of France: 20 French Melodies from the World. Les Compagnons d'Accordeon. Trace Trading
Heart of the Forest: The Music of the Baka Forest People of Southeast Cameroon. Track 4 and 5: Water Drums

Classical and Jazz Music CD'S

Copland Aaron. *I bought me a cat* from *Old American Songs* Bruce Hubbard, baritone. The Orchestra of St Lukes under the direction of Dennis Russell Davies.

Van Beethoven Ludwig. *Duetto buffo di due gatti* (Humorous duet for two cats), from *The Power of Song.* Felicity Lott, soprano, Ann Murray, mezzo soprano, Graham Johnson, piano.

Van Eyck Jacob. *English Nightingale* from *The Flute's Garden of Delights.* Marion Verbruggen, recorders

Ravel Maurice. *Ah! Quelle joie de to retrouver, Jardin!* (Ah! How much fun it is to find you again, Garden!) from *L' Enfant et les sortileges.* Berlin Philharmonic Orchestra. Simon Rattle, conductor.

Philidor Andre. *Gavotte des Festins* from *Marches, Fêtes & Chasses pour Louis XIV* played by "La Symphonie du Marais" conducted by Hugo Reyne.

Duke Ellington. *The Essential Duke Ellington. I let a Song Go Out of My Heart.*

Schumann Robert. *Papillons* Op.2 No 7: Semplice . Christian Zacharias (piano)

Saint-Saens Camille. *Introduction and Royal March of the Lions* from *The Carnival of Animals.* Ondrej Lenard and the Czechoslovak Radio Symphony Orchestra. Naxos.

Brahms Johannes. *Hungarian Dance No. 3* from *Hungarian Dances 1–21.* Hungarian Philharmonic Orchestra. Janos Sandor. Delta Music

ABOUT THE AUTHOR

Nicole Hammer taught music in Junior High and High school in Belgium and Preschool in the United States for 47 years. She studied at the Royal Music Conservatory in Ghent, Belgium earning a dual Masters in Music Theory and History. She has a diploma for Teaching Music from the Central Examination Commission in Brussels and is a certified Orff-Schulwerk teacher through the American Orff Schulwerk Association as well as a certified Montessori teacher. Nicole has presented numerous workshops for Preschool and Kindergarten teachers and written articles featured in periodicals such as the "Orff Echo" and various Montessori publications.